Farmhouse Witchcraft

Farmhouse Witchcraft

Penny Parker

Copyright © 2014 by Penny Parker.

Library of Congress Control Number: 2014902072
ISBN: Hardcover 978-1-4931-7021-0
Softcover 978-1-4931-7022-7
eBook 978-1-4931-7020-3

All rights reserved. No part of this book may be reproduced or transmitted in any form or by any means, electronic or mechanical, including photocopying, recording, or by any information storage and retrieval system, without permission in writing from the copyright owner.

This book was printed in the United States of America.

Rev. date: 01/29/2014

To order additional copies of this book, contact:
Xlibris LLC
1-888-795-4274
www.Xlibris.com
Orders@Xlibris.com
552927

Contents

Introduction 11

Chapter 1	Blessed beginnings..15
Chapter 2	Blessings for all things 20
Chapter 3	Spells and charms...31
Chapter 4	Crafting and gifts from the earth 75
Chapter 5	Recipes..101
Chapter 6	Alters and the season 123
Chapter 7	Which witch?... 125
Chapter 8	From my heart (pagan musings)......................... 133

This book is dedicated to my family, for without their love and support, I would not be the woman I am today.

My husband, Dwight

My daughters, Sabrina and Kari

My grandchildren, Austin, Andrew, Cassie, Meridith, and Parker

My mother, Elizabeth, and sister, Tea

In loving memory of Alic and Timothy. We lost you too soon.

What is a witch: A witch is a loving being with a heart of gold, a thoughtful soul, and a magical outlook on the world.

To be a witch is to grow into something better, stronger, and greater. As you change, so will your view on the world and your outlook in life. You may find yourself looking with new eyes to see things you never saw before. You may find you walk different, and bad habits start to fade away; or you may find yourself with less temper and a brighter outlook, and others around you will see the changes as well. So grab your broom and pointy hats, and let the magic begin.

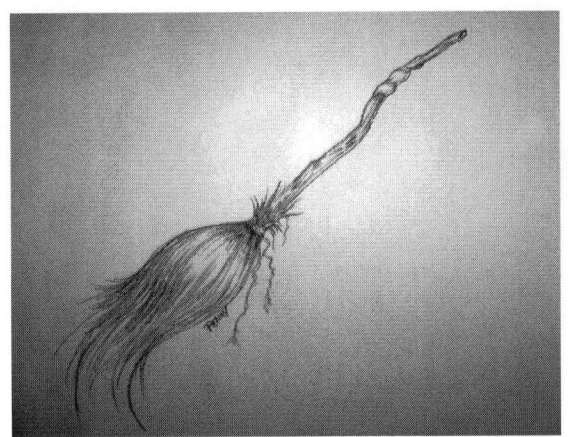

Introduction

Everlasting: Wind blows softly. Can you feel me?

Waves wash onto the shore. Can you hear me?

I am everlasting and always with you,

I hold you close as you sleep,

I am the rain that washes the tears you weep,

I am everlasting and always with you,

I am the sun that warms this land,

I am the strength when you are too weak to stand,

I am everlasting and always with you,

I am the dream you hold in your heart,

I am close though we are far apart,

If you cannot find me, look to the moon,

I wait for you love, to be with you soon.

I am everlasting and always with you.

—Pen Parker

After years of having been asked to put this book together and summers of dreaming as I work on our small farm, Witch's Hollow, tending my witches' garden, and posting on my site (The Good Witches Farmhouse Kitchen), my sister, Tea, with her Sabbath recipes and I with my spells, charms, and gardening tips, thinking of what friends and sisters would like in a book such as this, it came down to years of questions on why some books out there now seem to be hard to follow, and so many people asked me to make it simple and easy to follow. They asked me questions such as "Pen, why are some of the plants and herbs so hard to find?" "Why can't I use the plants on hand in my yard?" "Do I have to bless my candles only on the full moon?" "What if it's raining, how can the moon see what I put out?" And as more lovely friends, sisters, and brothers are going back to the old ways and learning about pagan/witch life, I say to you: well, it can be simple as I will go through in this book.

The tools of our craft are many, but in truth, we carry our power and magic inside us. It is our grace and our love that binds the power of our spirit. We all have our own gifts and use them for good or for evil, and yes, what we give out, we get back (be it good or bad). For light cannot exist with dark, for every action there is a reaction. We have our wands (yes, they have power) as do all of the tools of the craft, but self is the most powerful blessing of all. We call the elements and the moon and the sun to aid in our quest. Our intent is for good and healing. It is our intent that shines in the darkness and lights the way with our love for this world and all who dwell here. A simple word holds so much power and magic (always make your words soft and sweet, for you never know when you may have to eat them), and yes, a touch can heal or hurt as with a word spoken or whispered can bring a smile or a tear. Walk softly upon this earth, for every step will leave a print. It is my hope that the prints we leave are the ones of love and light, of goodness and kindness.

In days of old, the witch lived on the outskirts of many a town. We were the healers, the midwives, and the spell weavers; and in our small cottages, we used what we had on hand. There was no mail order, no Google We learned, and we made the best of what was on hand. As an earth witch, I use plants, trees, and herbs in my craft. As I do in the making of creams and salves, all things come from nature.

In this book, you will find a bit of history, blessings, how to make creams and healing salves, spells and charms, recipes for Sabbath, crafting tips, and using what is on hand. The witches of old had to be resourceful, and in this day and time, we also need to be resourceful. So let us honor the old ways and walk in the footsteps of the wise, put on your big witch panties, and let's begin our magical journey at the turn of a page.

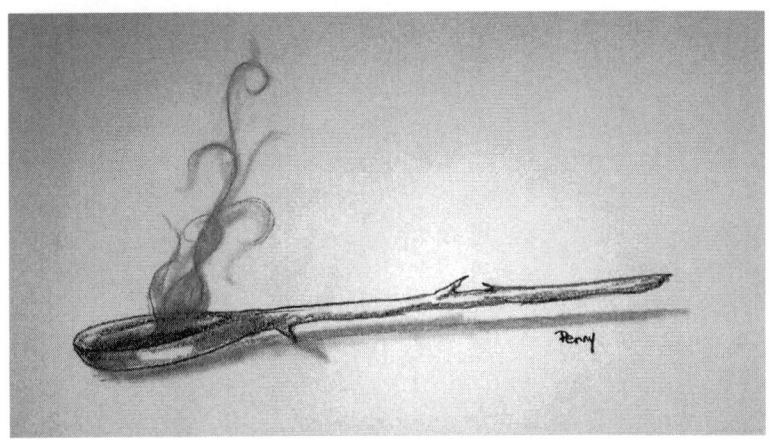

Chapter 1

Blessed beginnings

Look to the land, for it has all we need,

Give thanks to the land and all you see,

Set in rhyme your spells to learn,

For in our hearts the fires will burn.

—Pen

What is a pagan: Paganism is a religion of nature. Pagans revere nature. Pagans see the divine as immanent in the whole of life and the universe, in every tree, plant, animal and object, man and woman, and in the dark side of life as much as in the light. Pagans live their lives attuned to the cycles of nature, seasons, life, and death.

What is witchcraft: Witchcraft is an ancient craft and was known as the craft of the wise or the craft of the old ones because most that followed the path were in tune with the forces of nature, had knowledge of herbs and medicines, and were valuable part of the village and community, such as shamanic healers, leaders, and midwives. They understood that humankind is not superior to nature but is one with nature and all things.

What is Wicca: Wicca draws upon a diverse set of ancient pagan religion. The religion usually incorporates the practice of witchcraft. Developed in England in the first half of the twentieth century, Wicca was later popularized in the 1950s and early 1960s by Gerald Gardner. Gardner was a retired British civil servant and an amateur anthropologist and historian who had a broad familiarity with pagan religions, esoteric societies, and occultism in general. At the time, Gardner called it the witch cult and witchcraft and referred to its adherents as the Wicca. From the 1960s onward, the name of the religion was normalized to Wicca.

)O(Book of Shadows)O(

A bit of history of this is varied. Some Book of Shadows (BOS) are handed down through the ages while others are made by the new witch/pagan, but either way, this book is a part of you, the witch.

There are no set-in-stone rules on making your own, but there are guidelines.

Let's take a look at the book's history, lore, and legion.

Whether it's called a Book of Magic or a Book of Shadows, it's important for every witch to create a book of records. These are your personal notes, a diary of your spiritual or magical journey. A book to record your interpretations, aspirations, affirmations, notes, charms, and spells.

All right, all right, let's make this simple: It is a book kept and used by a witch to record research, thoughts, experiences, and spiritual information, such as spells, charms, incantations, potions, and so on. I have bits of plants and herbs pressed into mine and drawing of plants on the page that the spell was written on. As with all religious texts, debates loom about how the books came into use. Some say they were prevalent during the Middle Ages written only in runic alphabets to hide their magical meanings. It is widely thought that in the Middle Ages, many were illiterate, and the books did not come into practice until the fourteenth or fifteenth centuries. Even then, runic alphabets and codes were used to protect the owner from persecution and death if found by witch hunters.

Making a Book of Shadows can be as simple as a composition book or binder, or you can order one online (but they are pricy). One of mine is a hardbound journal that I added a bit of magic to by attaching crescent moons and stars. I have a friend that writes hers on index cards in a box. As with most of your magical wares, you will wish to bless your book.

Candles, candles, candles. Hmmmm, I think I will save that for later in the book!

Rhymes: spells, charms, and blessings

Most spells and charms are said in rhyme, as they are simple to remember this way, like the rhymes you still hear in your mind from childhood and songs. Writers still use this today to craft the music we play and can relate on many levels. Yes, you will find those spells take on a magical and musical quality when rhyme is used.

> *In the pages of this book you will see,*
>
> *I give my heart, a part of me.*
>
> —Pen

The moon and clouds, yes, it's a full moon, but it's so cloudy out there! Or it's raining so hard I do not wish to get my magical items all wet! So therein lies the problem! But our lovely and magical moon is still up there, so do not fret or worry. She (the moon) will still bless your treasured items, and remember, you have three nights to place your items out (the night before the full moon, the night of the full moon, and the night after the full moon). Yup, you have a bit of leeway there; and if it rains for three nights, just use a large ziplock bag and place them out there and blessed they will be.

Witchcraft has its dos and don'ts, and in all of life, what you give is what you will get. If you give out bad or evil, you will receive it back. Yes, karma can be a kick in the pants. Example: If one works a hex or sends a bad spell to someone, you shall receive the same back tenfold. Never work a spell in anger. Magic is not to be used in hate or malice, but with all laws come loopholes. Example: Someone sends you a hex. Well, you have the right to defend yourself and your loved ones by returning the spell to sender (reversal spell). It is just turning the tables, like a block in sports. Some call it the threefold laws.

As you journey deeper into the craft, you will see that all things came in full circle as in the wheel of the year or wheel of life. We are of the earth and are proctors of all that we see, each tree, plant, and animal, and should leave this world better than we found it.

The "wheel of the year" is a modern pagan term for the annual cycle of the earth's seasons. It consists of eight festivals spaced at even intervals throughout the year. These festivals are often referred to as Sabbaths; four of these fall on the solstices and equinoxes and are known as quarter days or lesser Sabbaths. The other four fall midway between these and are commonly known as cross-quarter days, fire festivals, or greater Sabbaths. The quarter days are loosely based on or named after the Germanic festivals and the cross-quarter days.

1. Midsummer summer solstice: June 20–23
2. Lughnasadh Lammas: August 1
3. Autumn equinox Mabon: September 20–23
4. Samhain Halloween: October 31
5. Yule winter solstice: December 20–23
6. Imbolc Candlemas: February 1
7. Vernal equinox Ostara: March 20–23
8. Beltane: April 30

Sigh . . . OK, now we have a bit of our history down. It's time to move on to the next chapter. See, that wasn't too painful.

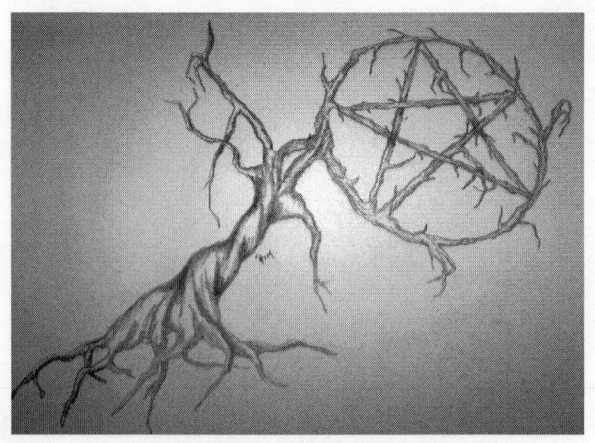

Chapter 2

Blessings for all things

This chapter is on blessings! Simple blessings that can be used in our daily lives, from our food to our candles and books. Yes, blessing (also used to refer to bestowing of such) is the infusion of something with holiness, spiritual redemption, divine will, or one's hope or approval. And in many cases, a blessing is to put our mark on something (to make it our own) as in blessed by my hand.

Example: Blessing your Book of Shadows to take an object of paper and make it divine and put our spirit in the pages and make this book blessed.

A blessing for your Book of Shadows:

A blessing of paper and ink to write,

Guarding this book with all thy might,

May the gods protect where this book does dwell,

For in it are many charms and spells,

For only a witch these pages will see,

This is my will, so mote it be.

Blessing a meal:

Blessed be the Earth for this food to eat

Blessed be the Sun for her warming heat

Blessed be the Wind and the life-giving rain

Blessed be the hands that helped plant the grain

For all the blessings we have this day,

Giving thanks to all is the witches way.

Meal time blessing 2:

Lady and lord, keep us safe, and bless us as we eat,

Blessing this meal, this bounty of earth, we thank you, so mote it be.

A candle blessing:

Candles of bright and shining light,

The moon soft glow and sun so bright,

A blessing of wax and wick I do,

These candles are now blessed, my powers are true.

Bedtime blessing:

Dancing shadows of silver light,

I lay my sleepy head tonight,

I awake to the sun's golden ray,

To start another magical day.

A blessing for a happy family:

By the love of Venus her arms open wide,

And the beauty of a rose that should never hide,

With the light of this home may love grow.

And bring blessings of love to all I know.

Moon blessing for a willow wand:

Wand of willow and moon's pure light,

By the powers of the elements on this magical night,

By fire, water, earth, and wind,

I ask for blessings of this wand by the powers you send.

Yule blessing:

Pine and holly, yule is in the air,

Gatherings of family, may all come out fair,

Blessings of love and light I give to thee,

Good well to all and many blessed be's

Fairies and winter

Fairies are pagan in origin and are found among the Celtic families. Once known as pagan gods and goddesses, the tradition to worship these little beings spread to France, Germany, and the British Isles. The Welsh peoples originally worked within a matriarchal society. They worshipped the Mother Goddess, and they called them fairies.

The Irish still say fairies live in the pagan sidh (burial mounds and barrow graves), several hundred of which still stand in the Irish countryside today. Fairies are also often found in wooded groves. Whether in hills or woods, mortals cannot often see fairies because of the division of the worlds; but every now and again, they get a precious glimpse of them. This often will happen at twilight, when the veil of the worlds is briefly parted. Throughout most of the former Celtic nations—Ireland, Scotland, Wales, Britain, and Germany—the fairies are becoming things of the past. Even though fairies are commonly believed to exist today, from the eighteenth century and on, they have been seen less and less. As most green witches, we protect the fairies; and in turn, they help us in our gardens as well as with our magic. We create fairies safe places for our friends, like fairies' gardens; and once you have the fay in your garden, magic will follow.

Those new to the craft should truly be thinking about making a fay garden, but be warned, do not underestimate them. Show respect, and you will get along fine.

The responsibility is great, for the fairies do not winter well, and many die off in very cold weather. You may see signs of the fay in your home, such as things misplaced. I have found that they get into my sewing things and play war with my pins and needles (they make swords) as I find them on the floor and other odd places. I had a friend who said they liked moving things, such as wrapping tape and string, but to have the fay in the house is worth it to me.

Tips for helping the fairies winter as the seasons change:

Invite the fairies in for the winter.

Bring in some green (houseplants and cut some evergreens). Make them feel at home.

Water and lightly mist your plants (the fay will feel like it is a spring rain).

Play music (the fay love to dance).

Feed the fay: Slice of apple with one drop of honey (not too much honey or you will have drunk fairies, and a drunken fairy is not a good thing).

Warning: When you change your greens for fresh ones, let the fay know (you do not want to toss sleeping fairies out [not good], so just let them know, and all will be well).

In exchange for opening your home to the fairies, they will aid in your crafting and protect your home and all who dwell there.

If by chance you have a wee child that is troubled by bad dreams, add some plants in the room, and the fay will guard the sleeping child.

Make life magical. Let your children and family help with a very fairies' welcome.

Charm to help bring in the fairies:

Warm home and heath I open to yea,

A welcome I offer to all you may see,

Making merry we will in this house filled with love,

As you hover below, between, and above,

Guard our home like your gardens is all that I ask,

As we go about our magical task.

Winter solstice blessing:

From the shortest days to the longest nights,

Winter solstice and magic so bright,

Renew the blessings and powers into me,

A gathering of love and hope round the yule tree.

Midsummer fairy blessing for the garden:

Oh my magical fairy friends,

I leave the spot for you to tend,

As this garden grows for you,

May magic make you strong and true.

As you tend this magical garden today,

Please know my love as you play,

And as you flutter about unseen,

May your garden always be lovely and green.

Seed blessing:

Grow the seed its life within,

Grow with love in the garden I tend,

My witch's work is never done,

As you sprout in the warmth of the sun,

My love of earth you will see,

Magically strong you will be.

Lammas blessing:

For love and comfort to all within,

Protection and care I do now send,

Herbs are drying and sun so bright,

A blessing of my home on Lammas night.

Lughnasadh blessing:

Late summers sun so bright in the sky,

This blessing at lughnasadh as birds flies by,

August bounty we give thanks to thee,

For all that we have and all that we see.

Mabon blessing:

September winds, come cool the air,

Lovely colors turning everywhere,

Mabon blessings I do send,

Good wishes to all family and friend.

Samhain blessing:

So cold the winds upon this night,

A chill does linger in candlelight,

A ghostly presents, you can feel,

Is this a dream, or is it real?

Footsteps fall, but on one is seen,

Blessings on this Halloween,

Shadows shift a silvery gleam,

The winds do blow a mournful sound,

The one so long ago in the ground,

Spirits visit on this night,

Pumpkins smile a frightening sight,

Witches dance as cat's eyes gleam,

Blessings on this Halloween.

Imbolc blessing:

The cold of winter winds do blow,

Imbolc blessing in the snow,

Brigit's gown of winter white,

Shinning softly in candlelight,

She brings with her the hope of winter's end,

Blessing to all we do now send.

Ostara blessing:

Ostara brings hope of the spring to come,

The warning of our golden sun,

Flowers blooms now scent the air,

The seeds we plant will come to bare,

The lamb and the chick are lovely to see

As spring fills our hearts for blessed we be.

Beltane blessing:

The greening of the trees and fields,

The turning of the great old wheel,

Yes, summers start the busy bee,

Blessing sent from me to thee.

....

As with all things, it is your intent. Words are just words, but we give them power.

The seasons turn with the wheel of the year on our small planet, and joy is to be found in all seasons as the gift of life, the budding of the spring trees, the planting of the seed, bubbling cool water on a summer's day, the bold colors of fall, and the restful blanket of the winter snow. Each season has its own beauty.

Chapter 3

Spells and charms

This chapter is, in my opinion, made difficult by many when it should be simple. As simple as we hold our power within each of us and can draw upon the green world around us in the fields and gardens, just a trip to the farmers market can be a powerful experience.

From the dandelion to the willow tree, there is magic! In the walk we take in the park and in the woods, each plant has a magical power. It's you who only knows what to look for, so let us begin on our journey into (the magic of the green world) spells and charms.

What is green magic, you ask? In green magic the witch becomes one with the (green) world. We use plants and herbs, trees and flowers; in other words, the witch acts as a bridge between the energies of the magical world and has the power to bring hope, healing, and love to the world.

What is a spell? Well, a spell is a spoken or written formula that when used in an act of magic is intended to cause or influence a particular course of events. Most spells are said in rhyme, and this makes it simple to remember, and most spells and charms are also said three times three, equaling nine. I find using a witch's rosary makes this simple, and you may make your own by using nine beads on a string and just running your hand over them as you repeat your spell/charm, then when you get to the end, you know it without losing count (simple). OK, enough of this and on to the crafting of spells and charms (I tend to get a bit long winded).

In this chapter, there are many spells/charms. Some are simple, but a few are a bit more advanced, and you may wish to wait to do them. Some spells use only (self), and some use plants and candles or a bit of string or ribbon. Always know it is your intent that marks a spell. In other words, if you flub the words, your intent will see you through to the outcome, so do not be frightened and remember that some spells may need to be repeated to gain the power to produce the wanted outcome (the more said and done, the more power to be done). Kinda like learning to cook. The first few meals may be OK, but as you learn and become stronger in your craft, you will be whipping up some yummy dishes with your eyes closed. Hmmmmm, I know I am being a bit long winded, or is it long winded when you type? Food for thought! Well, let's jump right in!

Deflection spell

You will need the following:

Fresh pine needles, red candle, and matches and candle holder (pine is for the planet Mars and stands for passion, bravery, aggression, and warrior, and the color is red.)

Place pine in a circle around the candle and light the wick (always do so safely).

Spell is said three times three.

Candle of red and pine so green,

Now set about in my magical ring,

I deflect all negativity at this hour,

As you surround me with you magical power.

Now let you candle burn out in a safe place, and place the pine out in your yard for extra protection.

....

Some spells are in the gray, and we as witches do have a divine right to defend ourselves and our home and family. A return spell is only sending what was sent to us.

Return spell:

As feather takes flight on this wild cold wind,

A reversal of sorts for the trouble you send,

Your untruths were spoken as malice dripped from your tongue,

My circle is cast, my spell has begun,

What was sent is now flying right back to you,

This spell is now cast, my powers are true,

No harm can you bring to me and mine,

Your malice and lies are now lost in the fabric of time,

I cast this spell by the powers of three,

This is my will so mote it will be.

....

A charm to clear your head:

You will need (well, only you!),

Whirling thoughts like the will-o'-the-wisp,

Lift this veil like the rising of a mist,

Answers to questions I ask of this spell,

A clearing of cobwebs may this turn out well.

....

Calming spell:

As the holiday rush sets in, take time for calming and grounding!

Needed: cauldron, pine and cinnamon, light-burning disk, and as it turns white, add a bit of pine and crushed cinnamon. Say spell three times three.

Winter winds of cold and ice,

Hearth of fire pine and spice,

This calming spell for all I see,

This is my will, so mote it be.

Remember me spell:

Out of the darkness, thoughts in flight,

Candle flame for remembrance this night,

Friends and love come what may,

In thy mind to remember this day.

Like flame to wick a light to see,

Though far away, remember me

As I will always be thinking of thee,

This is my will, so mote it be.

....

Healing spell using blackberry:

Healing blackberry your power be there,

Your healing powers with water fire earth and air,

Aid and speed the recovery of this wound,

Taking away the pain like the swipe of a broom,

I spin this spell in three times three; this is my will, so mote it be.

Full moon spell for lifting elusion:

Need: white candle

Light your candle and say the spell:

Clear as night and dark as day,

Still awaiting answers, but here I lay,

Moon's mysterious energies harken to me,

May this spell bring the power of prophecy.

This spell is cast, and my answers shall be found,

By the turning of the earth as the moon spins around.

Let you candle burn out in a safe place

Breaking a hex with garlic:

Need: a few garlic bulbs, black candle and holder (garlic is one of the most protective herbs)

Light your candle and place you garlic around it in a circle.

By the elements of earth, fire, water, and air,

I break your hex it is yours to bear,

Onto you as you did onto me,

A chant this spell by the powers of three,

The garlic's protection will send a reverse,

My home is now free from your dark curse

Let you candle burn out in a safe place, and the garlic should be buried in the four corners of your property as a barrier.

Breaking a spell that you have cast:

Well, let's look at this one. Hmmmmm, no one is perfect! And we all can make a mistake. I have had many friends call and say, "I found this spell on the web, and well, I did it, but now something is wrong." Well, it happens! And now let's climb our way out of this sticky web. Yes, it's like a spiderweb, and we are the fly.

Look at the web (or spell) and write it in reverse on a sheet of paper. You will need a piece of eight-inch thread (red is best) and a candle (black) with a good holder and matches.

Light your candle and hold the thread (one end in each hand) and say this charm.

Charm to break a spell: said three times three

Like the web of a spider the spell was cast,

But the hold of the spell will not last,

I undo what was done red thread in hand,

Now I break this spell where I stand, (break the thread)

What was done is undone for all to see,

This is my will, so mote it be.

Now say the (bad) spell in reverse and, when done, burn the paper to be rid of it . . . and let your candle burn out in a safe place.

Lost object charm

See in your mind a silver thread shining and bright; now see what you seek in your mind. Picture yourself with the silver thread in hand and your lost object on the other end and spin to draw it to you, coming closer as the thread wraps around, and you will see that was lost will be found.

Silver thread I spin to thee,

What was lost will come to me,

Silver thread shinning bright,

Lost object now found in my sight,

Silver thread spins around,

What I seek will be found,

In using what we have on hand, let's look to the dandelion (lion's tooth).

The dandelions (lion's tooth) are edible greens and source for spring tonic. The flowers make a dandy wine. The leaves are packed with vitamins.

Some of the folk names are blow ball, Lion's tooth, wild endive.

The root for the dandelion can be used to makes a lovely magenta dye.

Medical and magical uses are many and range from drinking as tea or carried in a bag to enhance psychic dreams, opening second sight, as friendship charms, and for ridding a unwanted spirit from your home. This is no common weed!

Traditionally, dandelions have often appeared in pagan rituals and are used on summer and fall alters.

The name dandelion is also for bravery and a strong heart. This plant is sacred to Hecate and planet is Jupiter. Element is air.

I always keep dried Dandelion root for emergencies.

Banishing a negative spirit/ghost with dandelion root

You will need one dried root of the dandelion and a cauldron or fireproof bowl and matches plus burning disk. Grind the root and light your disk. As the burning disk starts to turn white, sprinkle a pinch of the ground root (saving the rest) and say the spell (three times three).

This is a very strong spell; I would first try sage and or garlic. This is only to be used in extreme cases.

By the root of the lion and the magic of three,

I call now to Hecate and the power of thee,

Banishing the negative spirit I ask in my plea,

Leaving peace in this place, only love now to see,

Now remove the used disk and let cool and then dig a hole to put it in. Place in hole and sprinkle sea salt to seal. Cover with dirt. Now sprinkle remaining crushed root over the ground and repeat. This is my will, so mote it be. This spell is cast be the powers of three . . .

African violet

The lovely African violet is used magically to increase spirituality, to protect, and making a protection charm bag is a good way to use this small plant.

Protection charm bag:

Gather nine flowers from your African violet (please thank the plant for the gift).

You will need a small charm bag (you can make or purchase).

Sandalwood incense, lighter or match, and safe holder.

Light your incense. Place the flowers in your bag, and hold your filled bag over the smoke to bless.

Blessing charm:

I bless this bag and all within,

By the powers of protection it will send,

Protection seen and unseen held within,

Only love and light it will send.

Aloe vera

One of my go-to plants, aloe is a must-have! The aloe plant can be found in old Egyptian writings, where it was already being used as a healing plant. It has been called God's wand, heals all, to name a few.

Magical uses:

Protection

Luck

Water magic

Lunar magic

In addition to being a wonderful houseplant (a must in my kitchen), aloe is a powerful, protective herb. It keeps evil influences out of the home and wards off accidents. Grown in the home, it also attracts luck and prosperity to the home. Plant an aloe on the grave of a loved one to bring peace to the dead and the bereaved alike. Aloe is thought to relieve loneliness and is used in love spells.

Spell for luck:

Using dried and crushed aloe, burning disk, and fireproof bowl or cauldron, light the disk; and when it starts to turn white, sprinkle half teaspoon of your aloe onto it and repeat this spell.

Spell said three times three.

Magic aloe spell I spin,

Increasing luck do now send,

Good fortune and luck I ask of you,

This is my will my powers are true.

Let you disk burn out in a safe place.

....

Visions and dreams:

Visions and dreams and all things between. They may not be as they seem, for this you must trust your heart as you will not remember all; and before they wane in your mind, you should write them down (I keep a small book by the bed). As I wake, I try to jot them down. Dreams for the most part come to you while you sleep; though daydreaming as in deep in thought is a form of vision as you are awake, write them down also. Have faith in yourself and the dream world, and you will decipher the dreams and visions in time. You can open your mind in sleep with the aid of a spell (to see something that is blocked), but doing so, you must be ready (not all are meant to be seen) as the spell is advanced, and you will need to prepare yourself and what you will need. So I said have only cast this spell a few times, and it took its toll on my mind and body.

What you will need: (no subs for anything) If you do not have what you need, then put it off until you do!

Silver chain: this is needed to hold you to this world (like a lifeline).

Blue candle: is the sea and fire.

Incense and feather: for the air and earth (lavender scent please). It will aid in relaxing.

A sprig of lavender (it may be dried or fresh)

Gather the items you need. It is a good time for a ritual bath before you start. This is done at bedtime, so put on something soft you can sleep in. Now Light the blue candle (in a safe holder). Light the incense hole and the silver chain up your left hand and the feather in your right. Are you ready? Relax take a deep breath, and as you say the spell slowly, wafer the smoke of the incense to the silver chain and some to yourself.

Spell is said three times three.

Silver and fire shine your light,

Blue candle flame, calm sea tonight,

Lavender to relax your scent I partake,

As you aid me on the journey I must take,

Moon of dark and silver light,

You will lead me home before morning light.

Now in one breath, blow out your candle and make sure the incense is safe. Put the silver chain upon you neck (it will now be you true lifeline), for without this silver chain, there will be nothing to bring your mind back upon morning.

Yes, it's time to go to bed. Place the sprig of lavender under your pillow and relax. Close your eyes; think of a small boat made of a leaf with sails of shining threads, soft seas, moonlight, (just drift) hear the soft waves. Now think of what you wish to see and sleep; let the spell do its magic. When you awaken, write down all you remember (you may need to do this a few times). As I said, this one is a bit hard.

Cat's whiskers used in magic

Folklore has used cat's whiskers in good luck charms and wish charms. Never pluck or pull out the whiskers; let them fall out on their own! And if you have cats, you can find them lying about. Just pick them up and place them in a glass jar with a lid or stopper for later use.

In doing research for this post, I found that the cat's whiskers can be brought for a price, but I do not think this I wise (how do you know that the whiskers were not yanked out of the poor kitty), and then it could bring bad luck.

Using cat's whiskers to craft a good-luck charm is simple. Just add one whisker to a clay in any shape you like and bake (make sure you put a hook in the clay before you bake It).

To make your wishes come true:

Use three white candles (in safe holders) and your cauldron with dragon's blood scent and a burning disk.

Burning disk can be as simple as a piece of a charcoal brick (the kind used in grilling). Just let it turn white to be ready.

Light your burning disk in your cauldron and let it turn white. Light the three candles. Now crumble the dragon's blood and add one cat's whisker to the cauldron, and as the smoke rises, make your wish

The best wishes are not for self but for others.

Charm said three times three.

One whisker I do give,

One wish in smoke shall live,

Dragon's blood and fire flame,

_____ is the wish I do name, (fill in the request)

This spell is cast in three times three.

This is my will, so mote it be.

Now just let your candles burn out in a safe place and your cauldron cool down, then toss the ashes into the wind.

Binding

OK, let's take at look at binding. You can bind just about anything or anyone. Binding means what it implies (to bind, to stay, to keep). Looking at binding plants, you will find a long list, but not all binding is done with plants. Sometimes you will need a doll. Use a doll so someone will not speak of something you do not want told (a secret) perhaps or just gossip that can be harmful. Binding is used in love spells, and you can bind a spirit to an object until you can (banish) the said spirit or hold it forever bound.

To use a doll, you will need a few things, such as a small scrap of fabric, paper and pin, stuffings, and thread. Any color will do, but you will need red to bind the spell. Just sew the simple shape of head, body, arms, and legs and stuff with cotton or any natural filling. Write the name on the paper of the one to be bound and stuff it in the doll. Once this is done, you may work your spell. Using red thread sew, the xxx shape over the mouth of the doll and repeat you spell.

Doll binding spell:

I bind thee _____ to hold thee tongue,

I bind thee _____ my spell is strong,

No spite you speak, no whispered hate,

No harm shall come from this twist of fate,

Bound you are from speaking hate,

And bound you remain until I change thee fate.

Now place the doll in a box and store in a safe place. When you wish to remove the spell, just remove the stitches from the mouth.

Binding plants and trees:

Pine tree

Pepper

Wormwood tree

Ivy

Spruce tree

Bindweed

Morning glory

Most type of vine plant will do

Spirits can be bound in mirrors, but you must be warned and handle with care. If binding a spirit in glass, you will need salt and to dig a hole one foot deep. Lay the mirror in the earth, and sprinkle salt over it, then cover with soil.

I never do love binding spells. If love is bound, is it truly love?

Looking on to banishing plants and spells:

Banishing Plants

This is a small list of magical, hardworking herbs and trees used in spell work for banishing. Banishing is used to (remove) something or someone, be it spirits, trouble, or negativities. This covers so much ground! You can banish bad luck; banish that pesky neighbor (no, it does not mean your neighbor will go poof in a whiff of smoke, never to be seen again), but they will keep to themselves and stop bothering you! But never use banishing to harm (what we put out, we will get back). OK! OK! Let's take a look at the plants now!

Cedar tree

Cypress tree

Cloves

Sage

Fern

Mugwort

Yarrow

Solemn seal

Hawthorn berries and thorns

Rose or most plants that are prickly and have thorns can be used.

In most banishing spells, I use a white or black candle. If using thorns, push them into the wax, and you're set to do the spell.

Sage smudging works well as does just burning a simple black candle, but then you need that big pow, use the thorns.

Banishing spell:

Black candle, lighter or matches, thorns from the hawthorn or rose thorns, safe candle holder.

Light the candle and think of whom or that you wish to banish (this spell is worked at nightfall).

Said three times three.

Fire burns my candle bright,

Thorns of earth, banishing in the night,

Air to carry my spell so true,

Like ripples of water I banish you,

Harm me not, you and your spite,

I surround myself with protective white light,

By the power of fire I banish thee,

By the power of earth I banish thee,

By the power of air I banish thee,

By the power of water I banish thee.

This is my will, so mote it be.

Let your candle burn out in a safe place. Your spell is done.

This is a small list of witches' names for plants. In days of old, a healer could not let her mixtures be common knowledge as she would be at the least out of the healing and could be found to be a witch and put to death, so in those times, they made names to hide what was what.

Bone of an ibis: Buckthorn

Adder's tongue: Dogstooth violet

Titan's blood: Wild lettuce

Lion's hairs: Tongue of a turnip (the leaves of the taproot)

Man's bile: Turnip sap

Pig's tail: Leopard's bane

Hawk's heart: Heart of Wormwood

An eagle: Wild garlic

Ass's foot or bull's foot: Coltsfoot

Blood: Elder sap or another tree sap

Blood of Hephaistos: Wormwood

Burning bush: White dittany

Bread and cheese tree: Hawthorne

Blood from a head: Lupine

Bird's eye: Germander speedwell

Blood of Ares: Purslane

Blood of a goose: Mulberry tree's milk

Bloodwort: Yarrow

Blood of Hestia: Chamomile

Blood of an eye: Tamarisk gall

Blood from a shoulder: Bear's breach

Bat's wings: Holly

Black Sampson: Echinacea

Bull's blood or seed of Horus: Horehound

Bear's foot: Lady's mantle

Calf's snout: Snapdragon

Cat's foot: Canada snakeroot and/or ground ivy

Candelmas maiden: Snowdrop

Capon's tail: Valerian

Christ's ladder: Centaury

Cheeses: Marshmallow

Chocolate flower: Wild geranium

Christ's eye: Vervain sage

Clear-eye: Clary sage

Click: Goosegrass

Cucumber tree: Magnolia

Clot: Great mullein

Corpse plant: Indian pipe

Crowdy kit: Figwort

Cuddy's lungs: Great mullein

Crow foot: Cranesbill

Cuckoo's bread: Common plantain

Clear eye: Clary sage

Crow's foot: Wild geranium

Devil's dung: Asafoetida

Dragon's blood: Calamus

Dog's mouth: Snapdragon

Daphne: Laurel/bay

Devil's plaything: Yarrow

Dove's foot: Wild geranium

Dew of the sea: Rosemary

Dragon wort: Bistort

Earth smoke: Fumitory

Eye of Christ: Germander speedwell

Elf's wort: Elecampane

Enchanter's plant: Vervain

Englishman's foot: Common plantain

Erba Santa Maria: Spearmint

Everlasting friendship: Goosegrass

Eye of the day: Common daisy

Eye of the star: Horehound

Eye root: Goldenseal

Eyes: Aster, daisy, eyebright

Frog's foot: Bulbous buttercup

From the loins: Chamomile

Fat from a head: Spurge

Fairy smoke: Indian pipe

Felon herb: Mugwort

From the belly: Earth apple

From the foot: Houseleek

Five fingers: Cinquefoil

Fox's clote: Burdock

Graveyard dust: Mullein

Goat's foot: Ash weed

God's hair: Hart's tongue fern

Golden star: Avens

Gosling wing: Goosegrass

Graveyard dust: Mullein

Great ox eye: Ox-eye daisy

Hairs of a Hamadryas Baboon: Dill seed

Hair of Venus: Maidenhair fern

Hag's taper: Great mullein

Hagthorn: Hawthorn

Hare's beard: Great mullein

Herb of Grace: Vervain

Hind's tongue: Hart's tongue fern

Holy herb: Yerba Santa

Holy rope: Hemp agrimony

Hook and arn: Yerba Santa

Horse tongue: Hart's tongue fern

Horse hoof: Coltsfoot

Hundred eyes: Periwinkle

Innocence: Bluets

Jacob's staff: Great mullein

Joy of the mountain: Marjoram

Jupiter's staff: Great mullein

King's crown: Black haw

Knight's milfoil: Yarrow

Kronos's blood: Sap of cedar

Lady's glove: Foxglove

Lion's tooth: Dandelion

Lad's love: Southernwood

Lamb's ears: Betony

Little dragon: Tarragon

Love in idleness: Pansy

Love leaves: Burdock

Love lies bleeding: Amaranth/anemone

Love man: Goosegrass

Love parsley: Lovage

Love root: Orris root

Man's health: Ginseng

Maiden's ruin: Southernwood

Master of the woods: Woodruff

May: Black haw

May Lily: Lily of the valley

May Rose: Black haw

Maypops: Passion flower

Mistress of the night: Tuberose

Mutton chops: Goosegrass

Nosebleed: Yarrow

Old maid's nightcap: Wild geranium

Old man's flannel: Great mullein

Old man's pepper: Yarrow

Oliver: Olive

Password: Primrose

Pucha-pat: Patchouli

Peter's staff: Great mullein

Priest's crown: Dandelion leaves

Poor man's treacle: Garlic

Queen of the night: Vanilla cactus

Queen of the meadow: Meadowsweet

Queen of the meadow root: Gravelroot

Ram's head: American valerian

Red cockscomb: Amaranth

Ring-o-bells: Bluebells

Robin-run-in-the-grass: Goosegrass

Semen of Helios: White Hellebore

Semen of Herakles: Mustard-rocket

Semen of Hermes: Dill

Semen of Hephaistos: Fleabane

Semen of Ammon: Houseleek

Semen of Ares: Clover

Seed of Horus: Horehound

Sparrow's tongue: Knotweed

Soapwort: Comfrey or daisy

Shepherd's heart: Shepherd's purse

Swine's snout: Dandelion leaves

Shameface: Wild geranium

See bright: Clary sage

Scaldhead: Blackberry

Seven year's love: Yarrow

Silver bells: Black haw

Sorcerer's violet: Periwinkle

St. John's herb: Hemp agrimony

St. John's plant: Mugwort

Star flower: Borage

Star of the earth: Avens

Starweed: Chickweed

Sweethearts: Goosegrass

Tarragon: Mugwort

Tartar root: Ginseng

Thousand weed: Yarrow

Thunder plant: House leek

Tanner's bark: Toadflax

Torches: Great mullein

Tongue of dog: Houndstongue

Tears of a Hamadryas baboon: Dill juice

Unicorn root: Ague root

Unicorn's horn: False unicorn

Unicorn horn: True unicorn root

Wax dolls: Fumitory

Weazel snout: Yellow archangel

White: Ox-eye daisy

White wood: White cinnamon

Witch's aspirin: White willow bark

Witch's brier: Brier hips

Weasel snout: Yellow archangel

Wolf foot: Bugle weed

Wolf claw: Club moss

Wolf's milk: euphorbia

Weed: Ox-eye daisy

White man's foot: Common plantain

Charm for relaxing

A simple charm to relax and just be yourself using a white candle and your heart . . . Here is a charm for relaxing.

Charm said three times three.

Light your white candle and look into the warm flame and say this charm. It always works for me.

By the candle glow of warm white light

My troubles rise in the smoke of flight,

Calm and soothing relaxing my mind,

A simple charm said in loving rhyme,

Slowing and calming for thee to see,

This is my will, so mote it be.

Let your candle burn in a safe place.

Full moon spell for seeing the truth

Spell said three times three.

Need: full moon at midnight

Dark of night and rays of sun,

On this witching hour my spell has begun,

Earth, fire, water, and wind,

This spell of shadows I do now send,

Open eyes to see a sight,

Open mind on starry night,

Truth be told in lands of dreams,

All is not what it may seem,

To see the truth is all I ask,

To do no harm on this magical task,

Moons glow and stars so bright,

Open my eyes on this full moon night.

In times of Worries~

This is a charm that I use when I have worry and trouble or just need to be strong but feel weak. Just light a white candle, and say this charm in the morning . . .

Send the light to see me through,

Goddess blessing strong and true,

Dearest maiden, mother, and crone,

I know that I am never alone.

Magical Goldenrod

Goldenrod is often blamed for early fall allergies (ragweed's sins), but in truth, goldenrod blooms at the same time as the real culprit (ragweed).

Goldenrod is found most everywhere in the US. It is often seen along country roads, ditches, fields, and along the highway. Goldenrod is lovely when dried and used in fall wreaths and in sprays over the door.

Magical uses: lost objects, money, divination. To see your future love, when held in the hand, the flower nods in the direction of hidden or lost objects. Goldenrod is also used in money spells.

Spell using goldenrod: said three times three (nine) to find what was lost.

Goldenrod what lost is now found,

Magical powers spin around and round,

Golden light shine the way,

What lost will be found this day.

The dark days

As the dark day of winter lay heavy, at times, even the bright light of our upcoming yule cannot chase away the heavy dark mood. Lighting candles can add the warmth and bring light into the darkness to lighten the mood and heart, so when darkness beckons upon your life, take time to add candles and bring in light and love, warmth and life to the dark corners.

Start by a good tidying up the space you dwell (keeps you active), and being active will aid in dispelling the shadow hanging over you. Now add the light and warmth of candles (the more the better), and scented candles work best! Try making that fresh cup of tea or coffee (awaking the taste buds).

Bring in life by adding some evergreen, such as holly and pine. Just by doing these few things, you will start to feel more alive and brighter. There, now that's better! Do not let the darkness win! Fight! Yes, I said fight! For as always, there is battle between the dark and light! But by looking to the light and bringing it into your home, you will feel the darkness fade as the warmth and light bring life and hope!

Candlelight spell:

Need: white candle, match, and safe holder. Spell said three times three.

Candlelight and flame so bright,

Chase away shadows with all your might,

Darkness be gone, only light I see,

This is my will, so mote it be.

....

Simple truth spell

Let me see where I was blind,

Let the seal on my third eye unwind,

Separate the truth and lie that binds,

And show them to me in my eyes.

....

I find this little charm is helpful in my day to day life.

Banishing troubles:

May the goddess here my plea,

And bind up my troubles with all possible speed,

For in her light may trouble fade away,

Never to return on this day,

My troubles are bound by the powers of three,

This charm is worked, so mote it be.

....

Stay in the light:

As requested (in times of trouble and stress as malice touches out lives), stay in the soft white light:

Think of a white light surrounding you . . . It's peaceful and warm . . . and say this charm:

In grace I walk though a forest of thorns,

they reach to scratch but cause no harm,

protected I am by loving white light,

No dark can touch my path is bright.

Witch I am and witch I be

I proudly stand for all to see

My spell is cast no blood I used

For magic is my only fuse

For those who know me, know me well,

There is no evil in my spell.

Pet protection charm

Protecting of fur and feathered babies can be as simple as a charm or spell, and I have a very difficult spell; but when doing some, studying on the matter, I have made this simple charm today. I am using a small pentagram that will hook to Grimmy's collar (you may use a tag or anything that will hook onto their collar). Hold the item up and say the charm to bless it. I will also use blessed water and wash the item in it and a sprinkle on Grimmy's head to seal the charm, then attach it onto his collar.

Animal spirits of earth and sea

Of air and flame I pray to thee

Ancient spirits here my plea,

This creature I ask, protected be . . .

....

Dandelion root has been used in divination, wishes, and calling spirits and to open your eyes to untruth. I have used it in a simple spell to open my eyes to see truth from lies. This spell uses dried dandelion root.

You will need a dried dandelion root and a white candle. Lay your dandelion root on the left side of your white candle. Light candle (in a safe holder) and say the spell three times three.

My eyes are open to see at last,

Dandelion root, aid me in my magical task,

Flame and smoke part the veil,

Truth from lies will always tell,

Root and candle unwind the lies,

Truth is written on clear blue skies.

....

Binding evil: this spell is *not* for the faint of heart, and I would plead to you, the reader, to have at least three sisters or brothers with you when this spell is done! To bind evil or a dark spirit and hold it, then place it under the earth needs a lot of power.

A binding spell using pink knot weed:

First, tie a peace of pink knot weed into a knot and say this charm three times three.

To be protected from all you do,

This magic charm I cast on you,

With spoken words I bind thee,

For you to forever let me be,

To be protected from your harm,

Three times three I seal this charm.

Now take the knotted weed and dig down into the earth nine inches and place the pink knot weed in said hole. Sprinkle sea salt to seal it there and cover (do not look back). You may feel a pull to do so, but the binded will be fighting this, so do not look back! Turn and walk away.

Again, I stop to say as always: It's your intent that truly makes the spell.

Ridding yourself of darkness

Dark to light on this night,

Match strikes as flame burns bright,

Dispels the darkness and brings the light,

Dispels black thoughts with all its might,

As light burns bright upon this night,

As smoke and flame take the dark away,

Only light remains where I stay.

Thistle used to break a hex

Thistle has been long used in magic—for strength, protection, and hex breaking. Thistle can be carried in an amulet bag for joy, energy, vitality, and protection. In fact, men who carry thistle become better lovers (well, you will have to try that one)! Thistle can be burned as incense for protection and also to reverse hexes. Thistle makes powerful wands.

Spell to break a hex or return to sender spell

Said three times three.

Thistle blessed, strong and true,

I send your hex back to you,

The pain you have brought, you had no care,

Your hex is now your own to bare,

Thistle blessed protection circle me

And send the hex back to thee

This spell is said by the powers of three,

This is my will, so mote it be.

The sweet gum tree or witch's burr tree

This magical and protective tree has a five pointed leaf like the witch's pentagram and the fruit or gumballs called burrs, hence called witch's burr tree.

Used in protection spells that are designed to keep unwanted people away or in witch bottles because of their spines or burrs.

Early pioneers would scrape the bark and chew the resin. It has a protective and calming feel, good for inviting positive energies and keeping out the anxiety.

Wands for healing and protection can be made from sweet gum tree branches.

I use them in crafting and potpourri and my witch bottles. The burrs or (gum balls) keep unwanted visitors away.

Spell to keep unwanted guest away:

Spell is said three times three. You will need one witch's burr, burning disk, and fireproof bowl or cauldron.

First, grind the witch's burr into a curse powder. Light the disk, and as it turns white, sprinkle the burr powder on it and say the spell.

Pesky guest who causes unrest,

Witches burr will suite the best,

Linger at my door no more,

Your feet no longer at my door,

Fair-the-well I say to thee,

This is my will, so mote it be.

Sage to remove unwanted spirits and negativity . . . This is as old as time.

Need: sage and charcoal disc (you can use the kind for grilling, but the burning disk is best) or a sage wand, feather, and shell.

Before you start, close all of your windows, but leave one door open (the unwanted spirits will need an exit).

Start by lighting up your charcoal disc.

Wait until it turns white. That's when you know it's ready to start smudging!

Drop some slightly crushed sage on it and wait for it to start smoking.

When it starts smoking, go to each room and fill the room with the smoke.

While you are filling the rooms, you can inhale a small amount of the smoke to cleanse yourself.

As you step into each room and with a commanding voice, chant the following:

I cleanse this room of all negativity!

Only love and light may enter!

Pay attention to the smoke because when it turns black, it means that in that room, there is that certain negativity that you wish to dispose of.

When you went through all the rooms, return to the room where the smoke turned black and redo this until the smoke has turned back to grey!

To take an extra step, have all who live in the house to stand and blow the smoke from the sage over them (I will set smoking sage on the floor in a fireproof plate or bowl) and have them walk over it. At times it may not be your house that has attracted something unwanted.

One more step I use is to place a pinch of sea salt over doors and windows. You may also use salt water and write runes with your finger toward your home.

Garlic bulbs hung by the doors are good to keep nasty things out of your home, and placing a clove on each window is good too.

This is not a onetime thing; it will need to be done about once a month and, at times, back to back.

Common clover: As with the dandelion, this is not a weed, but a magical plant.

Clover has been used to protect against madness, strengthens psychic powers, and spirit magic, and associated it with their triple goddesses. This aloes brings to mind the old childhood rhyme:

One leaf for fame, one leaf for wealth,

One for a faithful lover,

And one leaf to bring glorious health,

Used to see fairies and other spirits, and of course, what child did not make a clover chain to wear! And placing a few of the flowers in the four corners of your home will keep evil away, but the clover has been mostly used in money spells; and as you will see from this book, I do not post money spells, as the goddess grants us the wisdom to know that we must work for what we need. If you do cast a spell for money, it will only come to you in small sums (you may be walking and find a quarter on the ground). Yup, you found money. If you wish to cast a spell to remove debt, I will tell you now that as we made the debt, the gods and goddess will want us to work to pay our own folly (no free rides).

Chickweed herb

Chickweed is not just a pain in the garden and should be shown a bit of respect, for it is a powerhouse plant (yes, yes, I know it takes over); but if you plant it in a spot (not in the garden) and let it run, it will provide much-needed healing. Chickweed has coumarins, rutin, B vitamins, iron, and saponins. Chickweed is best known for its ability to cool inflammation and speed healing for internal or external flare-ups. Chickweed tea is an old remedy for obesity according to Culpepper, and wise women and herbalists still drink teas of fresh chickweed as one of the classic spring tonics to cleanse the blood. Chickweed poultices are useful for cooling and soothing minor burns, skin irritations, and rashes, particularly when associated with dryness and itching. This just goes to show why outwinged friends like it so much. If this is good for them, then it is good for us.

Magically, it's a great addition to your cupboard. Its gender is feminine. The planet is the moon, and the element is water. Chickweed is often used in workings to strengthen or maintain a relationship or other rituals of love. It can be carried for the same purpose. While its area of concentration is relationships, chickweed can actually be beneficial in any lunar-based workings. Also, consider chickweed for animal magic or bird magic or when working with a bird totem or patron.

Try a moon spell using chickweed and the element of air.

Blessings of birds:

Wind to air, the rise of moon,

High above you swoop and swoon,

Blessed to fly above on wing,

Your lovely song on winds does sing,

Candle:

> I have been asked to give some info on the candle and color that any of us may need for wishing, blessings, charms, spells, and healing, so here we go!
>
> The color we use can make a difference in your craft, but please know that when you are not sure, use white (I do) . . .
>
> Black: Mystery (not evil) rids negativity or absorbs unwanted energy and releases it harmlessly.

Blue: Darker shades are good for growth, energy spells. Lighter blues are good for bringing peace and calm, soothing anger, and to repel the evil eye.

Brown: Used to connect with the earth, trees, and gardening and to promote stability.

Gray: Neutralizes negativity and removes it by making it inactive and to keep a secret.

Green: A healing color, it will aid in gardening and communicating with the fairy realm. Green will attract money, but only small sums . . .

Gold: Used to attract energy, health, power, and will draw money that is owed to you.

Orange: A balance of red and yellow, an orange candle will draw money, energy, and health.

Pink: Used for love, friendship, and to calm emotions.

Purple: Used to bring wealth, power, and honor and is good to repel slander.

Red: Used to attract lust and courage; aids in protection and force.

White: Protection and represents the divine spirit, health, and healing.

—Pen

Simple candle blessing that can be done anytime.

A blessing I do of wick and wax,

As I go about my magical task,

This candle blessing I lovely do,

Blessings for good my powers are true.

Charging your candle:

You should charge your candle before a ritual, and it will only take a few moments to do . . . Pick your color you wish to use in your craft.

You may start by personalizing the candle. You can add runes, names, signs, and words. Carve this into your candle.

Now to dress your candle: Hold your candle in both hands. With your right hand, rub your candle from the center upward to the wick and release. Repeat with you left hand but moving from center to bottom of your candle and release.

You should feel the energy building within the candle.

Oils and herbs can be used as you dress your candle. Your candle is now ready to use.

Closing on this chapter with the reminder as always: It's your intent that gives the power, and never cast in anger or with malice.

Chapter 4

Crafting and gifts from the earth

Lovingly crafting lotions and potions as gifts and healing salves is a magical way to say I love you to friends and family, and in this chapter, we will take a look at making use of what the green world gives us.

Cauldron bubbling and the scent of spice

Warmth of hearth of love and all things nice

Soothing salves to heal and cure

All gifts of this magical green world

Magic is in every plant, tree, and wild grass. From the smallest marigold to broad-leafed sage, healing, and soothing and stirred by your hand, let's jump into crafting lotions and potions.

Herbs for wound healing: This is a very short list of some that I use the most, but by doing a bit of reading, I am sure you will find a lot more plants to use.

Calendula:

The flowers of this colorful, sharp-smelling plant, more commonly known as the marigold, have long been used to speed up wound healing. You can apply calendula ointments or tinctures to minor wounds. If you grow marigolds, you should know that many of the plants labeled "marigolds" aren't actually in the calendula family.

Goldenrod:

Wound healing is one of the most common traditional uses for this yellow-flowered perennial.

Yarrow:

The Greek mythical hero Achilles used yarrow to stop bleeding in wounded soldiers, or so legend has it. Supposedly, this member of the aster family, formally known as Achilles millefolium, was named after him.

Aloe vera:

The sword-shaped leaves of this succulent plant contain a gel that folks have been using for thousands of years to soothe scrapes and burns.

Marshmallow:

Marshmallow is an herb that may be helpful in healing your internal wounds.

Slippery elm:

Slippery elm, also known as Ulmus rubra, is a species of elm tree native to North America that has been used to treat peptic ulcers, inflammation, and bronchitis. A member of the ulmaceae family, it tastes similar to maple syrup without the sweetness. The inner bark of the tree is used medicinally to help treat numerous health problems, including internal wounds.

Honey:

All honey has antibacterial activity, and each type of honey has different antimicrobial or disinfectant activity. Clean out your wound first with water or saline (salt water) or let the honey clean your wound. Honey quickly cleans, sterilizes, and closes wounds.

Gardener's hand cream

8 ounces pure coconut oil

8 ounces pure cocoa butter

15 drops of peppermint oil

1 ounce of beeswax

>Heat the cocoa butter, beeswax, and the oil in a double boiler until they are liquid. Stir with a wooden spoon to combine them.
>
>When melted and blended well, add peppermint oil and spoon into clean jars. Let cool and add lid!
>
>—Pen

Calendula/marigold healing salve

Used externally for burns and irradiated skin, bruises, soreness, and skin ulcers. I love to use it for cracked, dry skin, eczema, diaper rash, and garden hands. It can help reduce bleeding and is wonderful for sore nipples and varicose veins! In other words, this salve is good for almost everything! And is a *must*-have in my healing cupboard.

3 cups dried calendula/marigold petals

1 cup extra virgin olive oil, grape seed oil, or almond oil

2 ounces grated beeswax or beeswax pastilles

Optional: frankincense essential oil, 5 drops; tea tree oil, 5 drops

Cheesecloth

Heavy pot

Spoon

Measuring cup

Rubber band

Heat flowers in oil to a simmer (about 20 minutes).

Let the oil flower mixture set over night (the longer it sets, the stronger the salve).

Next, using cheese cloth over a clean cup or jar, strain the oil flower mixture (you will now have a lovely golden infusion).

In a double boiler, heat oil infusion and grated beeswax until melted and pour into clean jars and let cool, then seal (store in a cool dark place).

Magical uses: Being an herb of the sun, calendula can be used to remove negative energy. Oil can be used to consecrate tools, and the petals can be used as part of incense for divination.

The plant can be used in any ritual to honor the sun, as part of a sacred bath, incense, or strewing herb as well as to produce a yellow dye for and altar cloths for use in sun-honoring rituals. For protection, hang garlands of calendula over entry doors to prevent evil from entering.

Making salve from mugwort

8 ounces pure coconut oil

8 ounces pure cocoa butter

2 ounces dried mugwort

Crush your dried herbs lightly with your fingers to help them begin to release their oils. Heat the cocoa butter and the oil over a low to medium flame until they are liquid. Stir with a wooden spoon to combine them.

Add the dried herbs and simmer them in the oils, covered, over very low heat for no more than 15 minutes. Check the herbs after 10 minutes have elapsed to ensure that they do not burn. When the oil is fragrant and colored and the herbs appear parched and brittle, remove the pot from heat.

Strain the mixture through a cheesecloth-lined sieve into several smaller jars that have matching lids.

Allow the salve to cool uncovered until it becomes semisolid and is at room temperature. Screw on the lids. This mugwort salve, like others of its kind, can remain useful for up to five years.

Use your prepared mugwort salve by applying it directly to areas of irritated, swollen, burned, or wounded skin to promote healing and reduce the chance of scarring. It is also effective as a rub for tired, overworked muscles. Store it in a cool place away from excessive heat and light.

Jewel weed salve and cream (poison ivy antidote)

Jewel weed (touch-me-not) impatiens

This hardworking plant is very effective poison ivy antidote. The stem should be crushed and the liquid rubbed into the skin contacted by the poison. Jewel Weed usually grows near water or in shallow ponds. It is often found in areas where poison ivy grows. Jewel weed works well on burns, cuts, and bug bites and should be added to the healing cupboard.

Making salve from jewelweed:

6 cups fresh jewelweed coarsely chopped or jewelweed essential oil

2 cups good quality olive oil or grape seed oil

1 1/2 cups loosely packed grated beeswax (you can use more or less, depending on how thick you want your salve. If you add more, it will become the consistency of lip balm; less, the consistency of a jelly. This amount is somewhere in between).

Essential oils: Tea tree, lavender, and sweet orange if you wish!

And the following equipment:

Cheesecloth

Small pot

Strainer

Small containers to put your finished salve in.

Step 1

Chop up the jewelweed and add it to the pot. Add the 2 cups good quality olive oil.

Bring the oil to a simmer, and simmer the jewelweed for 1 hour until it is cooked down.

Let the oil cool and sit overnight

The next day:

Strain the jewelweed from the olive oil. If you have cheesecloth, this works best.

If using jewelweed essential oil, then skip step 1 and add oils and beeswax and any other oils you may wish.

Grate your beeswax and measure it out.

While you are grating, heat your jewelweed-infused olive oil back up. Add your beeswax. Stir until the beeswax is melted.

Once you are happy with your consistency, add about 20-30 drops of essential oil to make it smell nice and give it additional healing qualities.

Carefully pour your mixture into small tins. Let set until cool, add top, and store.

Store in a cool dry place.

Marshmallow salve:

Marshmallow root comfrey salve is great for your skin. The healing qualities of Marshmallow root are a powerfully soothing herb that combats infections, dermatitis and even varicose veins. Comfrey has been used since ancient times to repair body tissue and promote rapid healing.

To make the salve you will need:

1 cup grape seed oil

2 tablespoons comfrey oil

1 ounce dried marshmallow root

1 ounce grated beeswax

5 drops of sage oil (op)

5 drips of frankincense oil (op)

Combine the oils in the slow cooker and heat on low.

Add the dried marshmallow root and mix until the marshmallow is well coated.

Heat the mixture on low for approximately eight hours.

Strain the mixture into a heatproof bowl or pan (cheesecloth works best for straining out all of the solids from the oil). Clean the slow cooker.

Return the strained oil to the (clean) slow cooker and turn the heat to low. Add other oils and grate the beeswax into the oil and stir.

Once the beeswax is completely melted, give the mixture one more stir. Pour into clean, dry containers, and let cool (uncovered) until solid.

This is a must-have in my healing cupboard

Antiaging cream from the kitchen

This is the recipe I use for my skin care cream and a little about why I picked each ingredient and what they do to fight aging (wrinkles, dark spots, sagging skin). Why pay lots of money for skin care when it's simple to make your own? The ingredients are easy to find and work better than any product I have found on the market.

Recipe for face, neck, and hand cream:

As with any skin care product, always try a small amount on your arm first and check for allergies.

Ingredients:

1 teaspoon pure coconut oil

½ cup cocoa butter

1 ounce calendula oil (make calendula oil by infusing handful flowers in grape seed oil)

1 ounce beeswax

1 ½ ounce grape seed oil

½ teaspoon frankincense essential oil

½ teaspoon lemon essential oil

¼ teaspoon tea tree oil

1 ounce pure honey

Melt all ingredients in a bubble boiler over med heat.

Remove from heat when completely melted, and using a wire whisk, whip as it cools to a cream and spoon into clean glass jars. Store in a cool dark place. Use nightly after the toner I posted a day ago.

A little about the ingredients I use and how they work.

Skin care:

Honey:

When it comes to firming and tightening, honey definitely takes the top spot. Tried and tested, pure, raw honey has been used for years. You see, honey is jam-packed with vitamins, minerals, and even amino acids, making it one of the sweetest natural beauty products there is—literally and figuratively.

Lemon:

Lemon to tighten loose skin on face, lemon is a natural skin-tightening and has anti-inflammatory properties. Astringent properties will close open pores and refine course skin. This skin-tightening home remedy will remove dead skin cells and free radicals to help tighten skin pores.

Frankincense

Frankincense essential oil is great for skin care and nearly everything related to skin. Used for mature, premature aging and environmentally challenged skin.

Coconut oil:

Coconut oil acts as a moisturizer, antibiotic, antifungal, multivitamin, multinutrient and antioxidant.

Grape seed oil:

Grape seed oil has vitamin C and vitamin E and fight against aging in themselves. Grape seed oil is packed full of both.

Cocoa butter:

Cocoa butter has been shown to improve skin moisture retention and elasticity and is effective in easing skin problems, such as eczema or psoriasis, and has been used in beauty creams for hundreds of years.

Calendula:

Calendula flower or pot marigold is a great herb for skin care and has perhaps the longest history of use of any herb in skin care. Often used for dry or damaged skin. It has natural restorative properties that infuse the skin with a youthful glow. Calendula oil is also used to protect the skin from premature aging and thinning of the skin. Calendula is safe enough to be used on the delicate skin under the eyes to prevent crow's feet.

This cream has been working well for me.

Making your own toner (or astringent)

Making your own toner is simple. Let's take a look:

Witch hazel is excellent and inexpensive because of its antibacterial properties. Witch hazel is useful in treating acne-prone skin and gives a deep cleaning. Add a few other things and you get a lot of power.

Tea tree oil is an antiseptic and antifungal.

Frankincense is also a valuable ingredient in skin care products for aging and dry skin. It acts to aid in the reversal of aging.

Lavender used in toner adds antibacterial, antiseptic to the toner.

½ cup witch hazel (not the cheap kind it contains water)

5 drops tea tree oil

5 drops lavender oil

5 drops frankincense oil

Shake well before using. Add a small amount on a cotton ball and apply to face and neck (always test a new product on your wrist before applying to your face). Use at bedtime.

Making a gentle and healthy soap for the face that has the power to also fight signs of aging is simple and only contains four ingredients. I use this with the toner and cream I have posted. The soap is used day and night! The Liquid Castile Soap I get on Amazon for less than $10. You can make your liquid soap if you wish. Making the three antiaging products would make lovely gifts placed in a basket for yule.

Facial wash:

1 cup Liquid Castile Soap

5 drops frankincense essential oil

5 drops lemon essential oil

5 drops tea tree oil

Soothing softly scented spice lotion:

To make this you will need:

Two pots to create a double boiler

1 pound cocoa butter

1/4 cup Almond oil

2 tablespoons grated beeswax

2 tablespoons honey

2 tablespoons coconut oil

4 drops each of frankincense and orange oil

2 drops cinnamon oil

Op: I used a pinch of powdered cinnamon for a light color.

Measure out beeswax, fat oils, and cocoa butter and place it the top of your double boiler. Let this mixture melt and then add honey and stir in scented oils and (cinnamon coloring if you wish).

Let mixture start to cool (mixing every now and then). As it starts to thicken, it is ready to spoon into jars and use (my early post on the power of the oils). This lotion is very good for the skin (not for all skin types).

How to make you own healing lip balm:

What you will need:

1 cup of olive or coconut oil

1 teaspoon comfrey leaf (optional)

1 teaspoon of calendula flowers (optional)

1 teaspoon yarrow flowers (optional)

1/2 cup lightly grated beeswax

1/2 teaspoon grapefruit seed extract or vitamin E oil to preserve (optional)

5-10 drops peppermint essential oil for scent/cooling/soothing. It contains natural aspirin to heal the ruff, chapped lips!

(Optional) If making this for cold sore healing, then use five to ten drops of tea tree oil.

(Optional) If you want a bit of color in your mix, then add the stub of your old lipstick and let melt into the oils (I did mine a light pink gloss). PS: If using color, then hubby may want to forgo using your lip balm!

How to make healing lip balm

Infuse the herbs into the olive or coconut oil. There are two ways to do this: You can either combine the herbs and the olive oil in a jar with an airtight lid and leave for three to four weeks, shaking daily, or heat the herbs and olive oil over low heat in a double boiler for three hours (low heat!) Until the oil is very green. You can also omit this step completely or just a drop of each of the essential oils instead.

Strain the herbs out of the oil by pouring through cheesecloth. Let all the oil drip out and then squeeze the herbs to get the remaining oil out.

Discard the herbs.

Heat the infused oil in a double boiler with the beeswax until melted and mixed.

Pour into small tins, glass jars, or lip chap tubes and use on dry or chapped lips.

Indian spice bath powder:

You will need:

1 cup arrowroot (found in the spice dept.)

1 cup cornstarch

1 cup baking soda

1 teaspoon Indian spice tea (ground and powdered), 2 drops each of cinnamon oil, frankincense oil, and orange oil (you may also make this unscented).

Mix and jar. Add a bath puff, and this makes a lovely gift.

Indian spice room is so simple to make (just 16 ounces spring water and frankincense oil, orange oil, and cinnamon oil [four drops each]). Add a tablespoon of Vodka (to keep it fresh). Shake and place in spray bottles.

Indian spice bath salts:

Epsom salt (one four-pound bag)

1 cup powdered buttermilk

1 teaspoon Indian spice tea (ground and powdered)

4 drops of each—frankincense, cinnamon, and orange oil

Mix and place in pretty jars.

Use 1 tablespoon per bath.

Negativity dolls:

The creepy, wee things are very useful and can be found in history, though little is known of them. Found in tomes and old native sites, the dolls can be made of hides and stuffed with grasses and straw or made of cloth and stuffed with cotton, and more were made with pores clay. They were made to drink in the negativity in a home or dwelling and keep out bad spirits. You may have seen them in shops that sell new wave collectables or witch/pagan shops and thought, "That thing is so ugly. It's kinda cute." Well, they were made in twos and threes and placed in boxes until they were needed. Here's how they work:

Once made, place them in a box in a dark place until needed. To use the dolls, just remove from the box and set or lay it out, and the doll will drink up the negative energy from the room. In a couple of weeks, remove the doll and plant it in the soil about nine inches deep and sprinkle sea salt to seal the dark negativity in the growth. If you wish to keep your doll, just place him in a dish of sea salt. This will suck the negativity out of him. Toss the salt away when done.

Making blessed spices for your home:

Sage: Planet: Jupiter. Used for wisdom, protection, and healing to name a few.

Lavender: Planet: Mercury. Folk name: elf leaf. Uses are creativity, commutation, and intelligence to name a few.

Thyme: Thyme is the jack of all herbs and is best known for purifying but have many, many other uses.

Rosemary: Planet: Sun. Used in success, purifying, and achieving personal goals.

Nutmeg: Planet: Jupiter. Used in luck and strength to name a few.

Cloves: This is a hardworking spice and will do many things. It is used to drive away negativity and hostility.

Frankincense: Used in purifying

Cinnamon: This is a strong spice and will add a lot to spells and give your casting a big punch, and it has strong lasting powers.

Using you blessed spices:

Using mortar and pestle, crush each spice and herb (frankincense). Can be a stick found in the candle department.

Mix all herbs and spice and place in a glass container. Using a teaspoon of your mix and a burning disk, go to each room and say a small blessing.

Rid this home of all negativity, may only light and love remain,

Now your home is cleaned and blessed.

Making a house protection jar:

House protection jar items needed:

1 glass jar with cork stopper or lid (a small canning jar is fine)

1/2 to 1 cup salt (depending on size of the jar)

3 cloves garlic

9 bay leaves

7 tablespoons dried basil

4 tablespoons dill seeds

1 tablespoon sage

1 tablespoon anise

1 tablespoon black pepper

1 tablespoon fennel

1 bowl

In the morning, ideally on a bright and sunny day, assemble all items.

Place the salt into the bowl and say:

Salt that protects, guard my home and all within it.

Add the cloves of garlic to the bowl and say:

Garlic that protects, guard my home and all within it.

Crumble the bay leaves, place it in the bowl, and say:

Bay that protects, guard my home and all within it.

Add the basil and say:

Basil that protects, guard my home and all within it.

Add dill and say:

Dill that protects, guard my home and all within it.

Add the sage and say:

Sage that protects, guard my home and all within it.

Add the anise and say:

Anise that protects, guard my home and all within it.

Add the pepper and say:

Pepper that protects, guard my home and all within it.

Add the fennel and say:

Fennel that protects, guard my home and all within it.

Mix together the herbs and the salt with your hands. Through the movement of your hands and fingers, lend energy to the magical protective herbs. Visualize your home as safe, guarded, and secure Pour the mixture into the jar. Seal tightly and place in your home with the following words:

Salt and herbs, here my plea,

Guard my home. My family and me.

So mote it be.

....

Making cinnamon wish/spell disk

Pagans and witches alike have been making these lovely smelling wish/spell disk for many, many years, and using them is simple. Once you make some, you will fall in love with the scent and magic of the spell disk. You can use them in magic and hang them around your home for that lovely scent. Give them as gifts, and it's a good craft that the wee witches can help with! You just need a few things to start.

What you will need: (no glue in this recipe as the disk are made for burning)

Ground cinnamon

Unsweetened applesauce

Rolling pin

Cookie cutters

Making:

Mix unsweetened applesauce and ground cinnamon to form a thick dough. Sprinkle ground cinnamon onto counter (this will keep it from sticking) and roll out to about a quarter inch thick and cut with your cookie cutters (you may want to use something to poke a hole for hanging). Now place your spell disk onto a wire rack to dry (I have found that mine dry faster on top of the refrigerator. It's warm up there), but anyplace warm and dry will do (if you do not have a wire rack, use a cookie sheet; but it will take longer to dry, and you will need to turn them). In about a week, your spell disk are ready to use.

Using your spell disk:

You can make a wish and toss them into a fire for Sabbaths, or if using for spell work, you will need to scratch your needs on the disk and then crumble into the fire in your cauldron. Your spell/wish is carried on the smoke.

....

Medicine bag or spirit bag blessing

> Ya Ta Say (Ya a teh)—greetings from Witch's Hollow. Today I was asked how to bless a medicine bag or spirit bag, so grab your feathers and let's go
>
> —Pen

Sage blessing:

For driving out negativity and for healing, white sage is preferred, but any sage will do.

Sweetgrass is used for blessing after sage has been used.

It is an important part of Sioux and Cherokee ceremonies. Sweetgrass is braided like hair.

Blessing your bag is a simple process.

Gather your items:

Sage wand and, if you wish, sweetgrass, braid a feather, and a burning shell (any natural bowl can do)

Items you wish to place on the bag such as crystals, stones, shells, herbs and plants (I like a cat's claw in mine as cats walk in both worlds), a cat's whisker for stealth, pinch of sage for protection. You make the rules for your bag. It is a part of you.

When ready, light your sage, and as it starts to smoke, take your feather and wave the smoke on your bags and items to be blessed and then wave the smoke at yourself.

Burning sage is fire.

Feather is air.

The shell is sea water.

Again, sage is grown in the earth, so it is earth.

It is customary to give a pinch of tobacco as an offering.

Apache (hi-disho-it is finished)

....

Making and using a scrying mirror

Making your own scrying mirror can be fun (let's give it a try). First, let's find a frame! An oval frame is ideal, but any other shape is acceptable. Try to find a frame that has appeal for you. The frame must have glass and not plastic.

First: Disassemble the frame and clean the glass. (Windex) Paint this side with a thick black paint. Oil-based enamel seems to work best. I prefer the gloss black, but matte black will work well also. Apply several coats of paint until light will not pass through the glass. Hold it up to the sun or light. If you can't see through it, then it's ready.

At this stage, you may paint designs or symbols around the edge of the frame if you are artistically inclined.

Next: Assemble the frame with the painted side of the glass to the inside. The thicker the plate of glass, the deeper the mirror will appear.

A method is needed to hold the frame at a shallow angle to the vertical. Some frames have a leg on the back that will do nicely. Trimming the bottom of the leg will adjust the angle. An alternate method is to use one of the display stands used for plates.

You now have your scrying mirror; if possible, bless this under the full moon to get it ready for use. Scrying takes some getting used to, and at times (first times), it will show nothing, but keep trying as it gets better with use.

Your mirror can be used for:

contacting spirit guides

accessing knowledge

healing

divining the past, present, and future

ritual invocation and evocation

Always keep the surface nice and clean using alcohol and a soft cloth, and never use it for anything but its intended magical purpose (and remember, this is your mirror) for your use only.

When to use your mirror: Scrying at night, during the full or new moon, depending on the situation. The mirror can be used at any time but is stronger at the moon and night.

OK, let's scry:

Turn off all lights except the candles or moonlight.

Allow nothing to reflect in the mirror's surface. It should appear as a dark tunnel or window.

You can use one candle behind the mirror or one of each side of it.

I like to burn mugwort or sage while scrying, but any incense you like can work.

Sit comfortably in front of the mirror.

Close your eyes! Clearing your mind of all thought but your purpose.

When you are ready, open your physical eyes and gaze into the mirror; remain relaxed and blink when necessary. Relax your eyes but remain alert. After a while, the surface of the mirror will begin to change and fade; a dark mist will appear. Your inner eyes will now open, and the journey into the mirror begins. Remember that the inner eye sees inside the mind through the magical imagination. Most people, when scrying, do not see the images appear with the physical eyes on the mirror's surface but see within the mirror and in the mind's eye.

When you are done, take a deep breath until you feel you have completely returned. Now close your eyes and remember all you saw. It's a good plan to have your BOS to write this down into while it's fresh in your mind.

Making a witch's protection bottle

Witch bottles have been around for hundreds of years. Today the purpose of the witch bottle is to protect a person from negative energy or hexes. Objects like rusty nails, razors, pins, thorns, urine, blood, and hair from the person being protected are very good to use.

A glass or ceramic jar or bottle with a big enough opening to put the objects in it (a canning jar works well)

Witches burrs (gum balls)

Pins

Razors

Broken glass

Needles

Sharp splinters of wood

Hair, fingernails, or blood

Rusty nails

Protection herbs

Vinegar

Urine

Just about any sharp or broken and nasty rusted thing you can find.

First, place all the items in your bottle. With each object, visualize the bottle being infused with protective energy. The last items you add would be the blood (menstrual blood could be used) urine, vinegar, or hair and nails. Urine and blood symbolize yourself and will be the strongest item in the bottle, and I will be a connection to yourself. Now seal the bottle. Some use wax over the seal (black candle wax is best). Now plant your bottle about twelve inches and cover with dirt. If you live in an apartment, you can place the bottle in a box and place in a safe closet. As long as the bottle stays intact and doesn't break, it will work.

Magical Water/Holy

There are many ways to make your own magical waters as there are types of water used for blessings and spells, but all magical waters need to be blessed, purified, and empowered. There are some sites and books that make this seem hard, and it needs a lot of work (please remember, it's your intent not what you have).

What you will need: spring water, sea salt, glass and a glass bottle with a stopper, and a full moon (yup, that's it). Add the spring water to a glass (about sixteen ounces) and, using sea salt (about a teaspoon), sprinkle into the water, give it a stir, and while you are stirring, envision the power of the moon, her grace and protection. Pour the water into a glass bottle, and upon the full moon, set the waters out for her to bless.

Blessed water can be used for warding, blessing items, and just about anything you need a boost of power for.

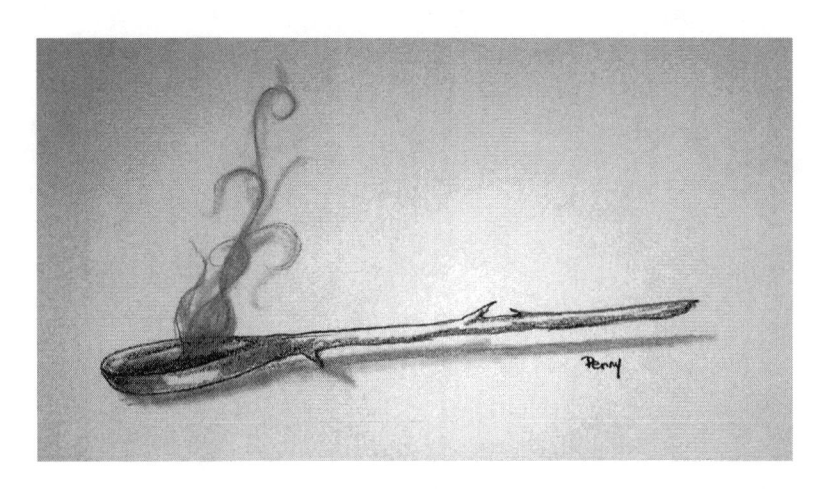

Chapter 5

Recipes

This chapter is some of my best-loved recipes. Most are from my family and have been used for years; some I have changed for this book as they were cooked on a wood-burning stove, and I thought most of you would not need to know how to bank your fires.

A thank you to my sister, Tea, who helped with the recipes.

Fall apple bread

1/2 cup unsalted butter

3/4 cup sugar or half cup Stevia

2 eggs

1 teaspoon vanilla

2 cups flour

1 teaspoon soda

1/2 teaspoon salt

1/3 cup milk

1 cup chopped cooking apples

1/3 cup chopped pecans

Preheat oven to 350.

Mix milk, margarine, and sugar. Add eggs and vanilla. Combine flour, soda, and salt. Add to mixture and alternate with liquid. Add apples and pecans. Turn into greased 9 x 5 loaf pan. Bake for about 1 hour at 350.

Apple cinnamon biscuit cobbler

4 apples—peeled, cored, and sliced

1 cup water

2 teaspoons ground cinnamon

2 tablespoons cornstarch

1/4 sugar

1 cup flour

1 teaspoon baking powder

1/4 cup canola oil

1 tablespoon honey

1/2 cup buttermilk

Preheat oven to 375 degrees Fahrenheit.

In a large saucepan over medium heat, combine the apples, water, cinnamon, cornstarch, and sugar. Cook about ten minutes until apples are soft and mixture is thickened.

Pour the apple mixture into a casserole dish.

Prepare biscuit dough by combining the flour and baking powder. Add the oil and stir until well mixed. Add the honey and buttermilk; stir with a fork until flour mixture is moist. Add additional milk if necessary.

Drop biscuit dough by tablespoons on top of apples. Bake for twenty minutes or until biscuits are golden brown. Serve warm.

Farmhouse Brunswick Stew

Makes eight to ten quarts, so it's good to freeze for a cold day!

INGREDIENTS

2 chickens cut up

salt and pepper to taste

4 large stocks of celery chopped

2 large onions quartered

4quarts water

1 20-ounce bag of butter beans

2 16-ounce bags of white corn

1/2 10-bag okra

2 1-pound, 6-ounce cans of tomatoes

3 large sweet potatoes, peeled and quartered

3 large white potatoes diced

1 cup ketchup

1/2 cup of vinegar

1/2 cup brown sugar

2 tablespoons Worcestershire sauce

1 teaspoon Tabasco sauce

1 teaspoon marjoram

1 stick butter

Place chicken in a large pot cover with water. Add salt, pepper, onions, and celery, and simmer until chicken falls off bones. Remove chicken; let cool and debone. Add remaining veggies and seasonings and until sweet potatoes are soft (remove sweet potatoes) and mash. Now return chicken and sweet potatoes to broth. Simmer for one hour until all seasonings are blended. The sweet potatoes will give a hardy thickness to the stew and a slight sweet taste. I make this every year, and it's truly wonderful.

Two of my most loved breads:

Samhain bread (Dutch oven): This yummy bread is simple to make and let rise over night

Ingredients:

3 cups unbleached all-purpose flour

1 teaspoon yeast

1 teaspoon salt

1 ½ cups warm water

Instructions:

In a large mixing bowl, whisk together flour, salt, and yeast. Add water and stir until a shaggy mixture forms (mixture will be loose and sticky; this is what you want). Cover bowl with plastic wrap and set aside for 12–18 hours (up to 24). Overnight works great.

Preheat oven to 450. Place a cast-iron Dutch oven with a lid in the oven and heat the pot for 30 minutes. Meanwhile, pour the risen dough onto a heavily floured surface (mixture will be sticky) and lightly shape into a round loaf.

Remove hot pot from the oven and carefully set in the dough. Cover and return to oven for 30 minutes. Then remove the lid and bake an additional 10-15 minutes. Carefully remove bread from oven and from pot and place on a cooling rack.

Iron pan corn bread:

1 1/4 cups milk

1 cup yellow cornmeal

1 cup all-purpose flour

¼ cup sugar

4 teaspoons baking powder

3/4 teaspoon kosher salt

2 eggs, beaten

1/4 cup unsalted butter, melted

1 tablespoon vegetable oil

Directions:

Preheat oven to 425 degrees Fahrenheit (220 degrees Celsius). Place 9-inch cast-iron skillet in oven to warm it.

Mix milk and cornmeal together in small bowl and let soak for ten minutes.

Sift flour, baking powder, and salt together in a mixing bowl. Beat cornmeal mixture, eggs, sugar, and butter into the flour mixture about one minute until you have a smooth batter.

Remove skillet from oven. Swish vegetable oil in the skillet to coat; pour off excess.

Pour batter into the skillet.

Bake in the preheated oven for eighteen to twenty-three minutes or until a toothpick inserted into the center comes out clean.

Farmhouse carrot cake:

2 cups granulated sugar

1 1/2 cups vegetable oil

4 fresh whole eggs

2 cups plane flour (not self-rising)

2 teaspoons baking soda

1 teaspoon salt

2 teaspoons ground cinnamon

3 cups raw finely ground carrots

4 ounces raisins

Preheat oven to 350 degrees Fahrenheit.

In a mixing bowl, mix sugar, vegetable oil, and eggs. In another bowl, sift together flour, baking soda, salt, and cinnamon. Fold dry ingredients into wet mixture and blend well. Fold in carrots and raisins until well blended. Fold into an oblong baking pan, which has been generously greased. Place in preheated oven, 350 degrees, and bake for about 30 to 35 minutes.

Icings:

1 1/2 pounds powdered sugar

12 ounces room temperature cream cheese

1 tablespoon vanilla extract

Farmhouse chicken and dumplings:

Ingredients

1 roasted chicken, cut up

6 cups water

6 peppercorns

1 tablespoon salt

1 teaspoon basil

1 teaspoon parsley

½ cup sliced carrots

½ cup diced celery

¼ cup chopped onions

Dumplings:

1 cup sifted all-purpose flour

1 tablespoon butter

1/2 teaspoon salt

1 egg, slightly beaten

2 tablespoons water

Directions:

Place chicken in a large pot and cover with 6 cups water. Add salt, peppercorns, basil, parsley, and carrots. Bring to a boil. Reduce heat and simmer for 1 hour or until tender.

Remove chicken and carrots from broth with a slotted spoon and set aside. Add celery, onion, and broth and simmer for 15 minutes.

While waiting, make dumplings. In a large bowl, combine flour, salt, and butter, mixing with a fork. Make a well in center of flour. Add egg and 2 tablespoons water and beat with a fork until ingredients are combined. Place the dough on a lightly floured cutting board and roll out until ¼ inch thick. Cut into strips, 1 inch wide and 2 inches long (I use a pizza cutter).

Bring broth to a rolling boil and add dumplings. Make sure dumplings do not stick. Cover and return to boiling. When broth returns to boiling, reduce heat and simmer for 10 minutes. Remove lid and return chicken and carrots to broth and simmer for 5 minutes. Ladle into bowls and enjoy.

Farmhouse sweet potato fluff

I have been making this for many years, and it is wonderful. I hope you and your family will love it.

3 cups sweet potatoes (mashed)

2 eggs (slightly beaten)

1 1/2 cups sugar

12 ounces condensed milk

1 tablespoon all spice

1 tablespoon cinnamon

1 tablespoon nutmeg

½ teaspoon baking powder

1 pinch salt

1 tub marshmallow cream

1 bag mini marshmallow

½ stick butter

Preheat oven to 350 degrees.

Mix sweet potatoes, eggs, sugar, milk, all spice, cinnamon, nutmeg, baking powder, butter, and salt.

Pour into a glass baking pan and add 4 dabs of marshmallow cream. Butter the stick end of a wooden spoon and lightly run it though the marshmallow cream. Do not blend; you want a marble look.

Now it's time to bake. Bake for about 45 minutes.

At the end of baking time, add the mini marshmallow and brown. Serve hot or cold.

Ham and bean soup:

1 pound dry navy beans, soaked overnight

4 quarts water

1 pound leftover ham bone with meat attached

1 onion, finely diced

2 carrots, sliced

2 stalks celery, diced

1/4 teaspoon ground black pepper

2 cups diced potatoes

dash of sea salt

In a large pot, add water, ham bone, and presoaked beans. Bring to a boil, reduce heat, and simmer until beans are close to soft. Remove bone and cut off remaining meat. Return ham and beans back to stock pot and add onion, carrots, celery, pepper, and potatoes. Salt to your liking. Simmer over low heat until veggies are tender.

Homemade chicken pot pie by Pen

1 pound skinless, boneless chicken breast halves

1 cup sliced carrots

1 cup frozen green peas

1/2 cup sliced celery

1/3 cup chopped onion

2 potatoes peeled and diced

1/2 teaspoon salt

1/4 teaspoon black pepper

1/4 teaspoon celery seed

1 quart chicken broth

Pie crust for two pies: I make my doe, but the store kind is good.

Cook chicken in chicken broth with seasons. When about done, add veggies (cook until tender).

Thicken with flour or cornstarch and set aside.

Roll out piecrust and place in the bottom of a pie pan.

Add filling (the chicken and veggies).

Place the second crust on top and press edges down (prick top of pie with a fork to vent).

Preheat oven to 425 degrees.

Bake in the preheated oven for thirty to thirty-five minutes or until pastry is golden brown.

Simple farmhouse rice pudding

2 cups cooked rice

1/2 cup sugar

2 eggs, slightly beaten

2 cups milk

1/2 teaspoon vanilla

1/2 teaspoon cinnamon (if you want)

Place rice in bowl. Add all ingredients and stir to mix. Pour into greased baking dish or pan. Bake for about 25 minutes in a 350-degree oven.

Can sprinkle with cinnamon.

Sweet apple buckle

10 apples

1 cup flour

3/4 cup sugar

1 teaspoon baking powder

1/2 teaspoon salt

1 egg

1/2 cup butter, melted

cinnamon to taste

1. Peel, core, and slice the apples. Arrange them in a 9 x 13 x 2-inch baking pan.

2. Combine the flour, sugar, baking powder, and salt in a medium-size bowl. Cut in the egg with a pastry blender until crumbly. Sprinkle this over the apples. Pour butter over top and sprinkle lightly with cinnamon. Bake for 45 minutes in a 350-degree oven.

Winter morning granola

This magical blend is a tasty treat on that cold morning. I make it early as to let the flavor mix, the lovely dried fruits, nuts, and oats. Make this a must for adding to my gift baskets. Tied with ribbon around a bag or placed in a pretty jar, I add a tag with the recipe on it so my friends and loved ones can make their own. Let's get to the recipe!

Ingredients:

10 cups rolled oats

½ pound of shredded coconut

16 ounces of chopped pecans

1 1/2 cup dark-brown sugar

1/2 cup honey

½ cup coconut oil

1 tablespoon vanilla extract

½ cup molasses

1 teaspoon salt

1 cup dried cranberries

1 cup dried blueberries

1 cup dried and chopped dates

Directions:

1. Preheat oven to 325 degrees Fahrenheit.

2. Measure the oats, coconut, nuts in a large bowl.

3. Combine the dark-brown sugar, molasses, and honey, oil, vanilla, and salt in a pot and warm up on the stove, stirring constantly. Then pour the hot mixture over the oat mixture. Stir well to ensure all of the oats are covered.

4. Spread the mixture onto a nonstick cookie sheets and toast in the oven for 1 hour. Remove the granola from the oven every 15 minutes and stir so that it toasts evenly on all sides.

5. Once cool, mix in the dried fruits.

Not just for mornings, it's a great snack anytime.

In the Celtic calendar, Samhain marked the beginning of winter and the end of summer. This was also the end of the third major harvest of the year.

Animals had been brought back down from the pasture to be housed once more in the barns and fenced in pens. Households had gathered in crops and preserved as much as they could for the coming winter months. Hay filled the lofts to feed the animals.

Some of the foods that would be in season this time of year include the following:

Fruits and vegetables

Beetroot

Brussels sprouts

Butternut squash

Jerusalem artichoke

Kale

Leeks

Parsnips

Potatoes

Sweet potatoes

Yams

Swede (rutabaga)

Turnips

Winter Squash

Apples

Pears

Nuts,

Chestnuts

Pecans

Walnuts

Meat and fish

Goose

Guinea fowl

Rabbit

Venison

Pork

Brill

Halibut

Monkfish

Mussels

Scallops

Swede chips

The humble swede, or rutabaga as it is called in America, can be mashed, roasted, or fried. We like turning it into chips.

Peel the swede and cut it into wedges about half inch thick and three inches long. Sprinkle it with olive oil and a bit of paprika.

Place it in on a baking tray and stick it in the oven 400 degrees Fahrenheit/200 degrees Celsius for about 35 minutes.

Root vegetable crisps.

What could be better for snacking on than a big bowl full of crisps? Make the crisps more interesting by cooking them yourself.

Thinly slice a variety of root vegetables. Some suggestions include beetroot, parsnip, swede, carrot, and potato.

Toss them in a bowl with olive oil and place in a single layer on a baking tray.

Bake in the oven at 350 degrees Fahrenheit /180 degrees Celsius for about 10 minutes. Check and turn them every few minutes.

When they are lightly browny, take them from the oven and season with sea salt. They'll crisp up as they cool.

Serve warm or let them cool and store in an airtight container.

Pork Roast

The general rule in our home is no pork unless the month has an R in it.

Even so, we tend not to have pork in months that don't contain an R in the name. Making this an ideal dish for autumn.

Autumn glazed pork chops

1. One teaspoon of olive oil in skillet. Heat over medium-high heat.

2. Sprinkle both sides of chops with pepper. Brown chops on each side in hot skillet.

3. Add apple cider. Cover tightly; cook over low heat for five to six minutes or until chops are just done. Drain off juices. In a small bowl, combine cranberry sauce, honey, orange juice concentrate, ginger, and nutmeg.

4. Pour over chops. Cook for one to two minutes until heated through.

Winter squash stew

1 tablespoon butter

1 large onion, chopped

2 pounds butternut squash, peeled and diced

1 large apple, diced

3 tablespoons whole wheat flour

1 1/2 teaspoons curry powder

1/8 teaspoon ground nutmeg

28 ounces low-sodium vegetable broth

1 1/4 cups whole milk

3 tablespoons grated orange peel

1/4 teaspoon white pepper

1/4 cup chopped parsley, optional

1 tablespoon grated orange peel, optional

1. In large saucepan, melt butter over medium heat. Add onion and sauté about 5 minutes until tender.

2. Add squash and apple. Sauté for an additional 5 minutes.

3. Add flour, curry powder, and nutmeg. Cook for 5 more minutes, stirring constantly.

4. Slowly stir in broth, milk, grated orange peel, and white pepper. Cover and simmer for 20 minutes.

5. In blender or food processor, purée soup in small batches until smooth. Garnish soup with parsley and orange zest, if desired.

Pear, apple, and cranberry compote

2 medium apples, peeled and coarsely chopped, about 3 cups (Fuji apples)

2 medium pears, peeled and coarsely chopped, about 2 1/4 cups (Bartlett pears)

1/4 cup apple cider

1/2 cup fresh cranberries

3 tablespoons brown sweetener

3/4 teaspoon ground cinnamon

1/8 teaspoon salt

1/8 teaspoon ground nutmeg

2 teaspoons fresh lemon juice

1 teaspoon Splenda® no calorie sweetener, granulated or you can use sugar

1/2 cup cold water

Directions:

1. Add apples, pears, apple cider, water, cranberries, sweeteners, cinnamon, salt, and nutmeg to a pot and bring to a boil over medium heat.

2. Cover, lower heat, and simmer 15 minutes or until fruit is soft. Remove from heat and mix in lemon juice. Serve.

This is a great topping for desserts or even as a sauce for turkey or ham.

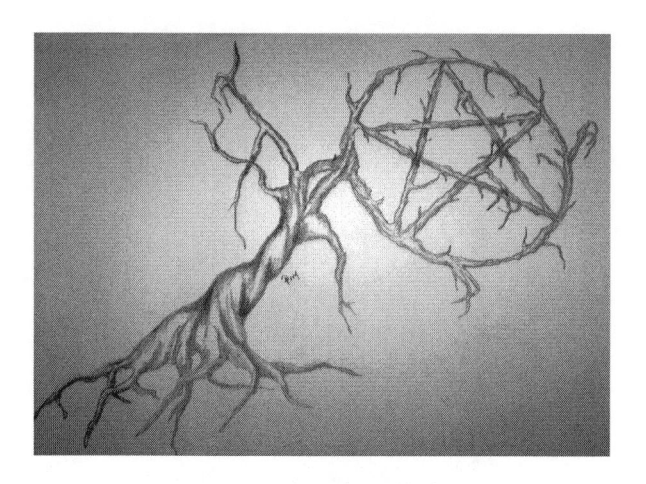

Chapter 6

Alters and the season

In this chapter, we will look at alters and the colors of the seasons, blessings of the fore major Sabbaths. Though this is not written in stone, and you may choose your own colors and decorations, this chapter can be used as a guide on crafting you own special alter magic.

Winter/yule alter and blessing:

I choose cold colors—blues, silvers, grays—but always bring in the solar aspect of the sun. This can be done by using crystals and sun catchers. This year, I will be using antlers and pine with candles in tall and short glass candle holders. Also, sparkling snowflakes will hang, and as the holly king battles the oak and the magical wild hunt, I will be adding a bottle of red wine, berries, and branches dry brushed with white paint for the look of show. A yule log with drilled-out holes to put candles can be done for those who do not have a fireplace or woodstove, but whatever you do, make it magical.

Winter blessing:

Short of day and cold of night,

As the wild hunt mounts for a magical flight,

Holly and oak I know we will yearn,

As we bless this magical winter wheel turn.

Ostar/spring:

Ostar is a celebration of the balance of light and dark that heralds the beginning of spring. Alters can be those early spring colors. Pastels are used the most on a spring alter as the trees start to bub and the yellow bells bloom to a soft green and warm yellow. The crocuses and daffodils peek their merry heads to wake the sleeping land. Pots of plants are good on a spring alter as they say rebirth of life. I like to make a clay baby lamb or chicks and some cuttings from the old yellow bell bush. Candles on the spring alter should be the same pastel colors. Crafting a most magical alter is simple as the waking nature gives us what we need.

Spring blessing:

Spring winds blow snow melts away,

Life renewed, warmth here to stay,

Birds herald, trees bud for all to see,

Spring blessing to all, so mote it be.

Chapter 7

Which witch?

Which witch?

As the wheel turns and times change, titles and labels are placed on just about everything, I have been asked many times: How do I know what kind of witch I am? In early years, there were two types of witches: light and dark, light casting only white, good magic and dark casting black magic. In today's world, you may meet a green witch or a kitchen witch. Another is the earth witch along with sun and moon witches, or you could run into an element witch, so many titles that it boggles the mind! So in this short chapter, we will go over a few and how you may (find yourself) in the witch mix.

The green witch or earth witch

How did I get to this wonderful place in life? The journey was not always easy, and my path was never straight. My early memories are of my mother out in her garden, working hard and taking time to have tea parties with my sisters and me. We would don our best dresses and make flower people and look for fairies in the rosebushes and ivy. My love for the green world and growing things marked my path in my early years, while in my teens, I found I loved lying under a tree, smelling the earth and moss, and listening to the slight sound of a whisper in the leaves (tree spirits whisper) and helping my mom pick mint and sage. Just the scent made me happy and peaceful. In my twenties, I would read every book I could find on plants, trees, and herbs, soaking in the knowledge like the green world soaks in the rain and sun; so many years later, I saw I was always a green witch (garden witch and earth witch).

The kitchen witch:

The bubble of something simmering over the stove, the scent of love filling the air as she stirs in magic to nourish those she loves. Do you love to cook? Like picking out fresh veggies and fruits, canning? Do wooden spoons make you happy? Why, you may be a kitchen witch! Grinding spices for blessing and cooking up magic.

Moon witch:

Does the moon call to you? Do you feel her pull so strongly it almost hurts? Then follow your heart and the moon. As she waxes, you feel yourself grow stronger (an opening of your third eye). In her full glory, you will shine and feel your heart melt into the silver glow of her power. As she wanes, you may feel the need to rest and refresh yourself, and in the dark moon, you can feel her ready to rise to her glory again. Moon magic is as old as time.

Sun witch:

She follows the sun with golden threads. A sun witch is a powerful healer indeed, for the sun heals the land and warms the earth (without blessings from the sun, our green world would be no more). The sun witch will use candles in her craft as the strike of match to wick, as the warmth of flame sparks to life, the sun witch spines golden magic.

Element witches:

Our four elements are a part of each of us. My element is fire, and the sun aides in my craft with the green world. Example: Fire (candle magic and earth), water may cast with the moon as she pulls the tides. Air may be pulled to cast her magic on the winds, birds, and candle (as the smoke from the flame carries her spell upon the winds). Earth will love plant magic and tree spirits. And *no*, I am not saying you are limited to only your element magic, but your element will make your magic stronger.

A bit about the elements and (witch) one you may be:

Water Element

Water element: Cancer, Scorpio, and Pisces

Water signs are attuned to waves of emotion and often seem to have built-in sonar for reading a mood. This gives them a special sensitivity knowing when to show love and heart at their best.

They are a healing force that brings people together. At their worst, they are psychic vampires, able to manipulate and drain the life force of those closest to them. Those with the water sign have to work harder than other elements to maintain their personal boundaries. Those with planets in water signs are often assessing a situation by its undercurrents. It can give them an air of being aloof or even shy at first, but they're the warmest of souls when you've won their trust. The feeling experienced by water signs can lead them into the arts. Some find release from their own personal dramas when they're able to express them as universal. As writers, musicians, and actors, they help others make sense of the human experience. But this also happens in everyday life since water signs soften the edges of the mundane by padding it with emotional meaning. Water is a formless element on its own, and that's why those with this sign are so quickly shaped by their relationships to others.

Water is associated with the direction west.

Water blue: Physical water, hydration, used for healing

Deep blue: Mental or emotional water

Blue black: Spiritual water, usually associated with buried unconscious issues

Water spells often involve liquid of some type, such as water, wine, or fruit juice. Pour the liquid you've chosen into a special goblet or chalice. Focus on your objective, mentally projecting your intentions into the liquid.

Water elements are normally very good at water gazing and or scrying.

Earth Element

Earth elements: Capricorn, Taurus, and Virgo

It's common to hear someone described as earthy. An earth element blends in with their natural habitat. They're sensual, meaning they engage with life through the five senses. Earth signs can operate at a slower, more thorough pace than the other elements. They're oriented toward what's real, and often this makes them very productive, able to see the fruits of their labor. But if there are no balancing elements, earth's extremes could lead to being a workaholic, hoarding of possessions, pettiness, getting stuck in mundaneness and stubbornness. Earth signs can just as easily work their magic in urban places since they're often centers of a certain kind of high-level productivity. The focus on the tasks at hand make them vulnerable to the all work and no play. Earth signs are here to shape, manifest, cultivate, and revel in earthly delights. Their gift to others is bringing form to ideas, making them a balancing partner for an idle dreamer with potential. They tend their own garden and inspire others to make the most of theirs.

Earth: stable, mass, rooted, and stationary

Positive aspect of the element of earth includes how it nurtures us, cares for us, and provides us with our needs. Working with the element of earth is strongly associated with agriculture and horticulture. Strong physical labor is enhanced by the element of earth associated to the world of animal life. Just like it does for mankind, earth nurtures and cares for all life. Physical sensations, the cycles of life and death, patience, steadiness, and well-being are traits all taught by the element of earth.

Colors of the earth element include brown, black, and deep greens.

Symbols for the element include the pentacle, salt, most rocks and gemstones, and soil.

Winter is the season related to the earth element.

Earth element presides over the North Quarter or compass point.

Using the elements of earth in ritual or spell casting: Using gemstones or crystals as focus of the spell or ritual will provide endurance and strength. Kitchen witchery or herbal magic is strongly associated with earthen elemental magic. Using the soil of earth to bury representations of problems will allow the elemental to slowly dissolve the situation away. Time heals all wounds, and earth is a master of time. Offerings to the earth will provide good health and long life.

Air Element

Air elements signs are Gemini, Libra, and Aquarius.

Those with planets in air signs use their minds to make sense of their lives. With air, there's more space between the life lived and the mind. This can lead air signs to appear distant detached, remote, and cool. Sometimes they'll try to talk their way through feelings or analyze a situation instead of encountering its full emotional weight. The gift of air is flexibility and their ability to experience life through many prisms. They're often excellent communicators, storytellers, interpreters, and writers and often have a curiosity that keeps them out and about. The air signs are social creatures. Air signs are more vulnerable to the excesses of our mind-body split, and meditation practice helps. Air signs calm the storm in the mind and sift through the rubble of their mind. They're great conversationalists because they're the keepers of so much knowledge, gossip, and strange facts. Air is the element of the east, connected to the soul and the breath of life. If you're doing a working related to communication, wisdom, or the powers of the mind, air is the element to focus on. Air carries away your troubles, blows away strife, and carries positive thoughts to those who are far away. Air is associated with the colors yellow and white and connects to the tarot suit of swords.

Air is associated with various spirits and elemental beings. Entities known as sylphs are typically connected with the air and the wind. These winged creatures are often related to powers of wisdom and intuition. Air elements manage the spells and rituals for travel, knowledge, freedom, openness, disclosure of lies, and so forth. The air can be used to open new mental abilities. Air manages magic four winds, predictions, and visualization . . . A few plants for the element air are broom, Catechu, citron, dandelion, dill, and lavender. Colors are of sunrise.

Fire Element

Fire element planets are Aries, Leo, Sagittarius.

Persons with fire signs have a simmering go-get attitude, as they hunt for things that light them up. They're prone to sudden illuminating flashes of insight. Like fire itself, they can flare up when inspired and making them seem very passionate about life. They like to live big and feel they can win any fight and often feel frustrated by mundane chores and duties.

Fire signs are known to be intuitive and to rely on gut-level feelings. Going on faith in their inner guidance gets them far, but they have a tendency to skip over important details or to be unaware of the emotional impact of their actions. Fire element act on instinct or sixth sense, and that makes them look reckless to more cautious types.

Fire magic is good for working on increasing one's activity for defensive magic, for protection, and, of course, for sexual magic. It can destroy, but it also purifies. It can help bolster courage and gets rid of negativity. As one would expect, fire plants tend to have a warm or hot taste (like chills). Fire scents are also warm. A good example being cinnamon or cloves, any spicy plants or tree will help in fire spell work. Other plants are stinging, thorny, hot, or stimulating plants.

Colors are also on the warm side of the color wheel in reds, oranges, and yellows. Fire elements love the sun and warmth and tends to get moody on days that are cloudy and dark.

Chapter 8

from my heart (pagan musings)

This chapter is close to my heart. This is my thoughts and musings.

Come Sit a Spell

Come sit a spell and speak with me,

My tea is warm and my friendship free,

Shall I read you leaves when you are through?

Shall I tell you all? Shall I tell you true?

Tell you true you ask of me,

My goodness, what have I put in your tea?

A wink and smile for you, my friend,

You time has come to a bitter end,

Did you not wrong me years ago?

In another life, you strung the bow,

You lit the fires that caused me pain,

Now your struggles are all in vain,

Witch you shouted in your strongest voice,

Come, come, let the poison run its course,

But how did I know who you are?

For I have looked for you long and far,

Ohhh, I could save you now, you see,

But I feel no love from me to thee,

The smile you had as they lit the fire,

You watched my suffer for over an hour,

Sigh, but a killer I am not so I give you your life,

Do not make me regret sparing you this night,

Harm none you will, your death I stay,

Do not make me come back another day.

A Walk Away

Breath held, she smiles though her tears,

Eyes bright she holds in all her fears,

Strong she always tries to be,

For weakness you will never see,

If she stumbles she will make a joke,

As tightness forms in her throat,

But freedom is a walk away,

In the sun she will spin and play,

Like the child she used to be

Making daisy chains and climbing trees,

Yes, freedom is a walk away,

For in the woods her heart will stay,

She unties her hair and lets it fall,

As she scampers over the garden wall,

Face turned up for the sun to kiss,

Closing her eyes in happiness and bliss,

Yes, freedom is just a walk away.

Child of the Moon

She walks so softly without a sound,

It is almost as if she drifts above the ground,

The trees bend their branches as she passes by,

And the stars sigh and twinkle from up in the sky,

The spirits in the woods watch her pass this night,

Fore a loving creature she is wrapped in bright light,

She finds the clearing stands so alone,

For in her heart she has come home,

The night animals gather, but no harm well they do,

Yes, her mother is moon, and her love pure and true,

Her mother the moon high above the mighty trees,

For she is one with the magic and blessed she will be.

Drifting

To feel the winds upon my face,

To feel no pain, not even a trace,

To drift in a dream this very night,

To drift in a sea where there is no light,

To close my eyes and just let go,

To float on the water as the winds do blow,

No thought to hurt my head do I feel,

Only the seas embrace is real,

Cool darkness closes overhead,

Or am I tucked safely in my bed?

....

Everlasting

Wind blows softly. Can you feel me?

Waves wash onto the shore. Can you hear me?

I am everlasting and always with you,

I hold you close as you sleep,

I am the rain that washes the tears you weep,

I am everlasting and always with you,

I am the sun that warms this land,

I am the strength when you are too weak to stand,

I am everlasting and always with you,

I am the dream you hold in your heart,

I am close though we are far apart,

If you cannot find me look to the moon,

I wait for your love, to be with you soon.

I am everlasting and always with you.

Flight of Dreams

Darkness comes a screaming night,

Frightening all there is no light,

I shiver in the cold to numb to move,

But I know in my heart what I must soon do,

My feet are bare as my toes find the edge,

I swallow my fear as I leap from the ledge,

Falling freely, my hair tangles and flies,

No fear now as I open my eyes,

In the blackness as form takes shape,

Wings spread I now see his face,

My dragon comes for me this night,

In dreams I fly this magical flight

Howl

The sound I hear, I have no fear,

Never far away, always near,

Whispered for my ears only you see,

Whispered in love from he to thee,

In sleepless nights I hear his call,

For in his arms I shall always fall,

Always in shadow he must hide,

Forever the laws we must abide,

For I am human and him not so,

But deep in the night our love will grow,

....

Let Me Fly

Unlock my chains let me fly away,

Let me spread my wings this very day,

Let me go, do not hold me here,

Do not watch me suffer what you fear,

I will come back as the wind on your face,

I will come back in the field where you pace,

I will come back in the shade of the trees,

I will come back as the soft summer breeze,

You will smell my scent in the spices of fall,

And know that I am with you through it all,

Just let me go, let me slip away,

For I will come back, and with you I will stay.

....

Never Alone

The word "solitary witch" implies that one is alone. As a solitary witch, I find this not to be true, for as a witch you are never alone.

Solitary Witch • • •

I have the sun to wake me and light my way (I am never alone).

As I walk the earth as my path (I am never alone).

The tree spirits greet me as I pass (I am never alone).

The wind whispers in my ear (I am never alone).

The rain washes away my tears (I am never alone).

The moon wishes me a good night (I am never alone).

God and goddess, lord and lady, we are never alone.

....

Old as Time

Of tails of old and story's told,

Of spells cast in silver moon and sun of gold,

Of yarrow and clover and said in rhyme,

Of eyes as dark and old as time,

Of book of shadows and feather quill,

Spells are cast in whispers still,

Of the ones before in dark of night,

Of the ones to come in brightest light,

All are sisters of the craft,

All will walk the chosen path,

Blessed are the witches, who walk in love,

As it is below, so it is above.

....

Passing

For you would not have seen me as I pass,

But for my footprints in the grass,

A trail to follow of rose and mint,

A trail nerveless though not heaven sent,

A human trail so long ago,

A trail that ended to soon, though,

Time is passing my footprints fade.

A life so short there was no trade,

Would I return if I could?

If I could come back, do you think I should?

But now I am free to blow in the wind,

Blessing to you I do now send.

....

Rest

Lay your head upon my breast,

And take you now your weary rest,

Peaceful dreams you will have there,

Silken dreams of long dark hair,

The calming scent of rose and mint,

In loving arms your sleep is spent,

Waking from a night so long,

Waking now the dream is gone,

But night will soon return so true,

In your dreams I wait for you.

....

Shadow

I am forever a shadow among candles so bright,

Never seen or heard, staying away from the light,

Never a sound do I make, for a shadow can give and never take,

I wander in darkness, unseen as I watch life go by,

My tears never fall as silent I cry,

Do you feel my cool touch as you pass on your way?

For I am with you always, by night and by day.

....

Singing Wind

I hear your call, in dark of night,

Spread of wings ready for flight,

Restless sleep I do wake,

For my love, this flight I do take,

My arms around your neck in trust,

My head resting this flight we must,

I feel my heart growing weaker this night,

As my dragon takes me on one last flight,

There at last this journey to end,

As you lay beside me, my love I send,

My eyes trusting, my blanket your wing,

A love never ending the winds will sing,

....

Spirit of the Earth

As the spirit of the dragon blows like smoke on the wind,

As the willow twisted and weeping in pain that never ends,

Like life-giving waters ripples and flows out to the sea,

As the fire of life in embers hiss a whisper let me be,

As the soil shifts and turns rocks tumble from above,

For the earth gives her children all of her love.

....

The Last Flight

Come thee, young one, fly high this night,

I shall take you there on this magical flight,

Hold onto my neck and have no fear,

For there is no room for worries or tears,

Hold tight to my neck and close your eyes,

For all have told you, your last goodbyes,

I take you to Summerland a place in the sun,

Where you will run with our forefathers and have so much fun,

We will touch the stars and fly past the moon,

Come thee, young one, I will get you there soon,

Your loved ones will follow in their own time,

I will bring them to you. This promise of mine,

A dragon's word is an honor, you see,

As this gift of a flight from me to thee,

Come thee, young one, our journey begins,

One old as time that has no end.

....

The Light

Whispers in darkness too soft to hear,

Binding shadows I show no fear,

A shiver, a chill runs down my spine,

The chill of the unknown forever entwined,

But the candle burns from within my heart,

Warming the chill and lighting the dark,

A tiny glow but if one looks one can see,

For the light of life burns within me.

....

The Love of a Witch

Shadows deepen, impending night,

Waxing moons power glowing bright,

Stronger she spins, her magic to see,

As she looks to the light and the power of three,

She calls to the elements as she cast the spell,

Silent is the night where the good witch will dwell,

Her eyes shine softly, like warm candle glow,

Even dragons calm to the love she does show,

Trees spirits bend their branches to see,

The love of a witch, blessed all will be.

....

The Mirror

Mist and mirror and candles burn,

Waning moon and spells to churn,

Vision clears to see at last,

Vision clears to see the past,

Mirror, mirror black as night,

Images faded come to light,

Waning moon, spell so true,

I must now say goodbye to you

....

The Power of Love

Love can light the darkest night,

Making it brighter, chasing away the fright,

Love's power reaches far across the land

It picks us up when we cannot stand,

Love crosses rivers and seas of blue

Always there, constant and true,

Love floats in air the feeling it gives,

Love is a power as long as we live.

....

The Winds of Past

So cold the winds upon this night,

A chill does linger in candlelight,

A ghostly presents, you can feel,

Is this a dream, or is it real?

Footsteps fall but on one is seen,

Shadows shift a silvery gleam,

The winds do blow a mournful sound,

The one so long ago in the ground,

....

The Wishing Fire

Fire blazing a most magical sight,

Lighting our lives and making them bright,

This witches fire on the ritual night,

Blessings and wishes cast into the light,

Love is sent as the smoke rises high,

Greeting happy spirits who wonder close by,

Wishes of healing and bright blessings too,

Sending love and light to all good and true,

As the embers glow, she is happy but spent,

May all be blessed by the love she has sent.

Waiting

A heart as cold as ice can burn,

For her lovers touch she yearns,

In the fortress of gray cold stone,

A tear is frozen for him alone,

Her icy hands blue from cold,

Still she waits for her lover to hold,

A thousand years frozen in place,

Cold and alone, but still she waits,

Like marble she is, frozen in place,

Her lovely eyes and her cold sad face,

But he never comes, as time goes by,

He cannot come for long ago he died.

Wings

Beating of wings tattered with age.

Fluttering too long in a gilded cage,

Letting go of fear held to long,

Letting go of hate that was so strong,

Open the door do not fear,

Open the door so all can hear,

Spread your wings, feel the wind,

Feel the love the earth does send,

Feel the rain upon thy face,

Reclaim thy life in the human race,

But frightened she whispers, I was too long in my cage,

For it is now my tome, my only stage,

For those who hold too tightly you see,

Like the bird in the cage will never be free.

....

Words

Words of hate do they speak,

Tears of pain I do weep,

A voice, a sound so painful to hear,

The weight of harsh words a burden to bear,

Soft words should be spoken of love and light,

Soft words should be spoken to make our world right,

If love was spoken in the world today,

It would take all the pain and wash it away,

Mind your words; Make them soft and sweet,

For you never know when those words you will eat.

....

You Do Not See Me

You do not see the pain inside,

You do not see the tears I cry,

You only see the smile I show,

My soft words are all you will ever know,

You do not know how short life is,

You only know the love I freely give,

You do not see my heart beat slow,

I will not let you watch me go,

Alone I will walk into the night,

But I leave you love and all things bright.

....

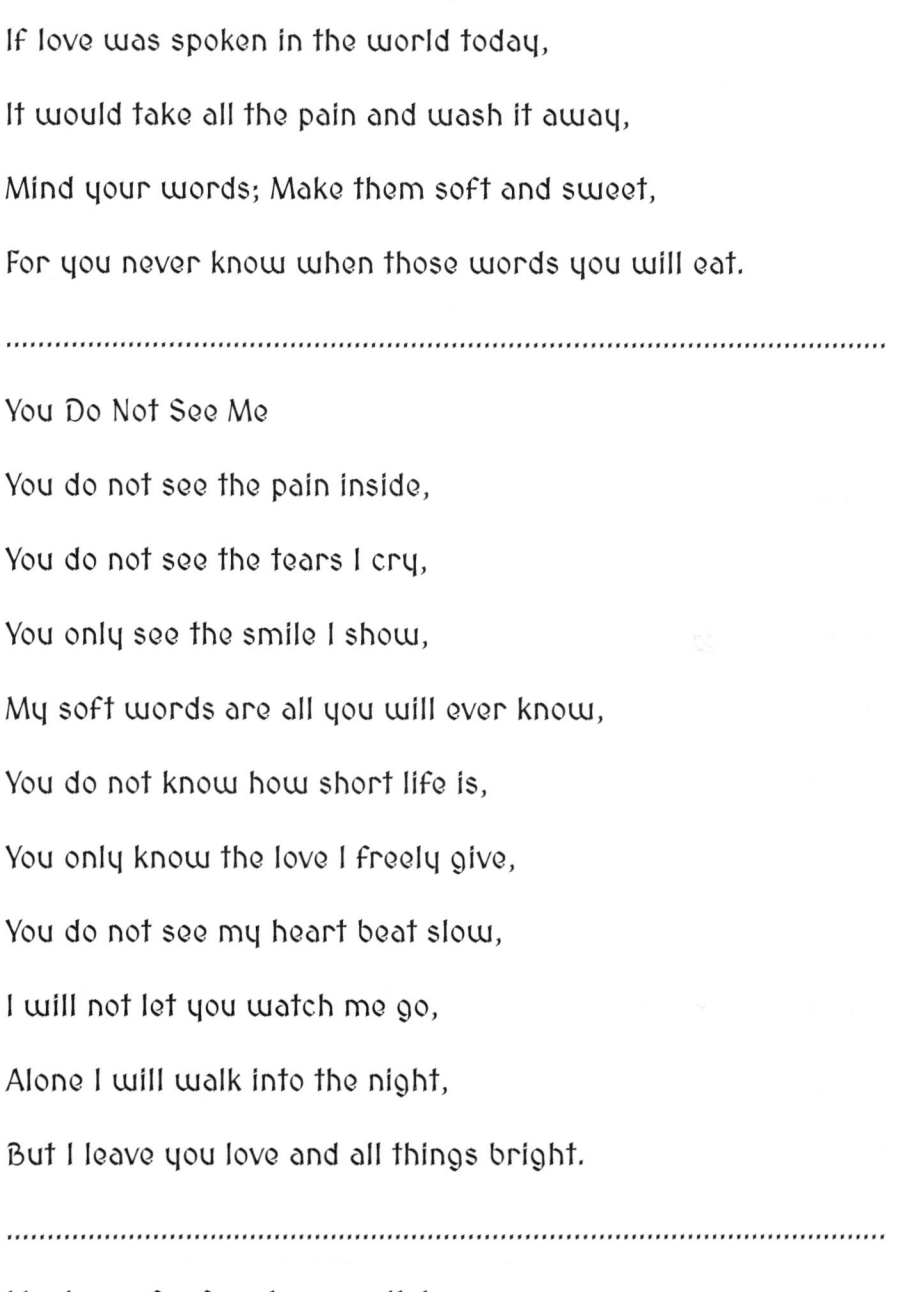

Musings of a farmhouse witch

As a green witch, gardening is a way of life to me, to feel the soil, scented and earthy, to dig, to plant the seeds of life, the harvest, and can the foods grown by hard work and, yes, sweat! Even the deep-seeded pleasure to prepare what I have grown from the great earth. Yes, gardening is a way of life, and at this day and time, it can also be life or death. I am what some may call an old soul. I heat with wood and hang my washing out on the line. In turn, I have a power bill of roughly about $50 a month and the best scented laundry from the winds and sun that dry it. Lots of fruit trees and berries in the summer and nuts in the fall. Yes, an old world life I live. I am not that fond of TV and much prefer to read a good book by the fire in winter and, in summer, to set under a tree and draw or read. I do have the web, but if not then, my small world would still be lovely and continue on in its slow rotation.

Yes, my life is simple and magical. Today the strong winds of January whip the sheets on the line. The pups are tucked into their spots just resting and awaiting a walk. Later, when they see me gather my basket and coat, they will head for the door prancing and hopping, ready to go. On my way to the woods I will stop by the herb garden and pick a bit of rosemary and a sprig of catmint for the kitties later (the kitties love it). In the woods we shall look for fern and moss, pinecones, and other lovely and needed things, and I will thank the earth and the Gods for each gift, talk to the sleepy tree spirits and let them know they are loved. After dinner tonight, I will flip open garden seed books and dream of spring, of planting time, and the great wheel. Yes, life is good

....

Musings of a farmhouse witch (summer)

As summer sun shines upon Witch's Hollow, I find a slowing of time. Yes! Time seams to pass with a slow tick of a unseen clock as the great wheel of the year turns to lazy hot day and softly scented summer nights. Summer has such a musical sound. The cicada sing of the joy of the green world. The humming of the bees and the sounds of tree frogs calling to their mates.

I feel so blessed as I go about my summer chores. Today is another canning day of tomatoes still warm from the sun and cucumbers ready to pickle as I open my cupboard and look at the bounty of jams, jellies, and pie filling all ready for fall cooking. As I walk out this morning to gather blackberries, I can see the blueberries are starting to turn a lovely color, and they will be next in the canner (blueberry pie filling). Yes, life is magical, and I am blessed to live it, to be one with the green world (in perfect love and perfect trust). My eyes and heart open to the joy of life and the sounds of the cicada summer song.

Musings fall

Bringing down the fall blankets and confuters, as I open the packing bags, I catch the scent of fall, a spicy smell of cloves, and cinnamon—a comforting and embracing scent of the linen bags I filled when I packed them up. I sigh with pleasure and place the scented linen upon the bed, and I know I will dream of warm fires in the hearth and sweet spicy breads in the oven! This is just what I needed today! A day of dreams, a day of pondering, the changing of the seasons, I find it is now not a chore but a blessings as I go about my work and I dream!

Musings of a farmhouse witch

On this cool October morning, coffee in hand, we went for a drive in the county and to the flea market. I look for what calls to me, and on this cool crisp morn, I heard a very large basket call my name. As I ran my hand over the worn old handles, I could picture in my mind this well-used basket being filled with piles of greens fresh from the fields, ready to be washed and looked and then the hearth wife (steaming pot) lovingly cooking the Sunday meal! Moving on and studying all the goods for sale, I spotted an old cider jug (what stories it could tell). Did it hold apple cider or spirits? When running a hand over this jug, I find that I see it on a worn wooden counter with others of its kind awaiting use from the good wife as the cookhouse fills with the scent of apples being pressed for the cider her family will be drinking. My other find this day is an old blue canning jar. This jar has the bubbles in the glass and still has the lovely old lid and seal in place. On touching the old jar, I see it ready by the hearth awaiting the goodwife to fill it with the harvest of fall apples peeled and sliced (I can smell the spices she will add). Yes, a trip to the flea market can be magical indeed.

Musings from a country witch

As thanksgiving closes in, my menu is planned, and it's time for me to start looking to yule, though I have already started the gift buying, and some new yule decorations are in the making. Little things like "Where am I putting the tree this year?" are nagging in the back of my head. This year's yule will be for the fairies and the colors of a cool blue and silver. But I need to set aside some me time, a time to walk and gather pinecones and berries, a time to relax and enjoy the winter season, the scent of cinnamon and cloves, the fun of making yule cookies and hot cider, a warm blanket on the porch with hot cocoa, watching the pups running the squirrels back up the trees.

Yes, 'tis the season, then life turns to warm fires and shawls, cold noses, and frosty hands and feet. As I type this, I look out the old French doors to see the red birds on the feeders and wet leaves drifting gently to the ground. Life is a grand magical journey, and it can be too easy to miss one moment of joyful bliss; for in a blink of an eye, it shall be gone.

May the glow of your candle warm and light your way.

May your days be blessed and beautiful.

And may all your winter dreams come true.

Loving light . . .

Musings fall

As the great wheel turns to fall and a chill comes in the air, the fields are resting from summer planting, and I look back on the summer and smile to myself on all that has been done. The drying of herbs and flowers, the canning of jams, jellies, and so many vegetables all ready for winter. My witch's cupboard's full and the healing herbs ready for use if needed, the wood cut and stacked ready for the colder days and nights. I think of the long walks to come and watching of leaves turning from green to gold as they softly flutter to the ground as if waving goodbye for now, of apple cider and hot cocoa, of soft hats and mittens. Of the scent of soups and stews simmering on the stove and warm bread with melting butter and honey dripping, of cuddling in warm, soft blankets and bonfires. Yes, life is magical indeed, so make it count as the wheel turns.

Musings of a farmhouse witch (summer)

As the dog days of summer hang over Witch's Hollow, canning season has begun. Tomatoes still warm from the sun await their turn for the pressure cooker. Some will just be peeled and canned. Some will become salsa, and others will be pasta sauces, and some will be eaten fresh picked. The first gathering of spring, herbs and flowers have been dried and bottled for healing, cooking, and crafting. With so much rain this spring and summer, I have lost some of my herbs. I could be upset, but I look to this as the green world telling me that it's time to reconfigure, rethink, and replant what was lost; but it is still heartbreaking as I remove a plant. The plants are like trusted friends who have given so much. I look at the lavender so sad, the stems blackened by rot, but I know the cutting I took from her and potted will serve just as she did. The lavender and many others will be recycled in the compost and will give a new start to life in the garden. All things in life recycle in some form. I have been crafting most of the summer making soap, bath powder, lotions, candles, and room sprays. Wreaths are made and awaiting fall. They have been scented with cloves and cinnamon oil and placed in large bags as when I take them out, the scent of fall will fill the house; but for now, I shall be content to plan and create as I look to the hazy summer sky. Yes, the dog days of summer hang heavy over the green world.

Musings of a farmhouse witch (summer)

As July wanes, I look to August and the last of the growing season. This has not been the best year for our gardens. The life-giving rains have been near every day, and we have lost a lot of plants to rot; but looking to the good side, our berries are fat and plentiful. The wines on Witch's Hollow will be good with many bottles of fine, sweet wine. I dream of fall now, of warm days and cool nights, of fall walks and turning leaves as the last of summers harvests are cleared from the fields and pumpkins are sat on the old porch to welcome visitors to come in and sit awhile in one of the rocking chairs and watch the pups chase the falling leaves. Life is magical.

Musings of a farmhouse witch

As another cloudy day forms in the sky above, my spirits are a bit low. For my element is the sun, it is hard for a sun child to thrive though so many dark days. I gather my pups and head outside, walking with purpose to the woods. I look up at the silver-gray sky as I make my way across the small stream that will lead me and the pups to the deep woods, and as I start up the path to the pine trees, I find the sun (yes, the sun!) in the form of a most magical gift of smiling bright-yellow daffodils, and my spirits sings and my day brightens. As I stop to pluck a few for the house, the pups are racing about among the bright gifts. I think such a small thing to some can be a gift of gold to me. And as I place the lovely flowers in an old blue jar, I know that today I can do anything I set my mind to do; but in truth, I think I will paint! And yes, my sun's gift will be next to me in the studio.

And with this chapter, we come to the end of our journey and will hold you no longer.

May your life be truly blessed in your magical path.

Research:

Buckland's Complete Book of Witchcraft

The Good Witches Farmhouse Kitchen on Facebook

Facebook Page Penny Parker

Book of Shadows by Penny Parker

....

Resource and supplies: 13 Moons.com (*http://www.13moons.com/*)

Made in the USA
Middletown, DE
07 November 2014